ENDORSEMENTS F

HeartLift confronts, discusses, and provides healing answers to the secret matters of the heart that leave it weighted with doom and gloom. Jill Morikone shares candidly the pain of personal struggles and those of other Christian women. She tackles the stumbling blocks of bitterness, failing to forgive, fear, and pride with a Christ-centered approach that will bring healing to the hurting places of the heart. With thought-provoking honesty and insightful wisdom, Jill offers practical steps toward surrendering to God's transforming love. This book will inspire and encourage you to trust the hand of God to give your heart a lift.

—SHELLEY QUINN, AUTHOR
AND 3ABN PROGRAM DEVELOPMENT MANAGER

Jill Morikone's *HeartLift* is a delightful example of "companionable writing"—stories and experiences meant to be shared from person to person, believer to believer. Some authors confront us, challenge us, and irritate us. But just as she does in her *Adventist Review* column, Jill opens her heart as we walk with her through the everyday hurts and joys of Christian living. Her courage, her hope, and her confidence in her Savior make this volume one that women everywhere will treasure and turn to often.

—BILL KNOTT, EDITOR
ADVENTIST REVIEW AND *ADVENTIST WORLD*

ABOUT THE AUTHOR

Jill Morikone, and her husband, Greg, are blessed to work at Three Angels Broadcasting Network (3ABN), where Jill is administrative assistant to the president. Jill is a church pianist and has recently completed her first piano album, *Father, Lead Me Home*. She enjoys spending time with family and friends, sharing the Word of God—especially with women—and writing. Her column, "Journeys With Jesus," appears in the *Adventist Review*.

3ABN BOOKS is dedicated to bringing you the best in published materials consistent with the mission of Three Angels Broadcasting Network. Our goal is to uplift Jesus Christ through books, audio, and video materials by our family of 3ABN presenters. Our in-depth Bible study guides, devotionals, biographies, and lifestyle materials promote whole person health and the mending of broken people. For more information, call 618-627-4651 or visit 3ABN's Web site: www.3ABN.org.

JILL MORIKONE

Heart Lift

EXPERIENCING
GOD'S FREEDOM

Pacific Press®
Publishing Association

Nampa, Idaho | Oshawa, Ontario, Canada
www.pacificpress.com

3ABN | books

Cover design by Ariel Warren
Cover image by Svetlana Christian
Inside design by Kristin Hansen-Mellish

The author assumes full responsibility for the accuracy of all facts and quotations as cited in this book.

Unless otherwise noted, Scripture quotations are from The New King James Version, copyright © 1979, 1980, 1982, Thomas Nelson, Inc., Publishers.
Scripture quotations marked KJV are from the King James Version.
Scripture quotations marked NLT are taken from the Holy Bible, New Living Translation, copyright © 1996, 2004, 2007. Used by permission of Tyndale House Publishers, Inc., Carol Stream, Illinois 60188. All rights reserved.

Additional copies of this book are available from two locations:
Adventist Book Centers®: Call toll-free 1-800-765-6955
or visit www.adventistbookcenter.com.
3ABN: Call 1-800-752-3226 or visit http://www.store.3abn.org.

Library of Congress Cataloging-in-Publication Data:
Morikone, Jill, 1978-
  HeartLift : experiencing God's freedom / Jill Morikone.
     pages cm
  ISBN 13: 978-0-8163-4677-6 (pbk.)
  ISBN 10: 0-8163-4677-1 (pbk.)
  1. Christian women—Religious life. 2. Emotions—Religious aspects—Christianity. 3. Mental health—Religious aspects—Christianity. 4. Seventh-day Adventists—Doctrines. I. Title. II. Title: Heart lift.
  BV4527.M637 2013
  248.8'43—dc23
                              2013033067

13 14 15 16 17 • 5 4 3 2 1

DEDICATION

To my best friend on earth, my husband Greg:

Because you—
Have loved God above all else
Have lived out your faith
Have walked in grace and integrity and humility—I trust you.

Because you—
Have loved me no matter what
Have encouraged my dreams
Have listened and cherished and protected me—I love you.

Because you—
Have prayed when the conflict grew fierce
Have led when a coward would quit
Have sought God's will above everything else—I desire more of
    Him.

Thank you for showing me Jesus!

ACKNOWLEDGMENTS

MY SAVIOR AND LORD—for searching for me until You found me, for picking me up when I stumbled, for cleansing my heart—I love You. For teaching me how to walk, for transforming my heart, for filling me with joy—I praise You. You are my hope, my joy, my everything. Because of You, I write.

GREG, my precious husband—thank you for asking me to share your life, for seeking God's heart above all else, for encouraging me to serve the Lord Jesus. You have picked me up when I wanted to quit, rearranged your schedule so I could have time to write, and been there each step of this journey. Without you, I couldn't have written.

MOM AND DAD PENNEY, my parents—thank you for teaching me of Jesus, for training me in the Word, for revealing the transforming grace of Christ in your lives. Because of your example, I've desired Him too.

MOM AND DAD MORIKONE, my parents, as well—thank you for raising a man of God to walk through life beside me, for showing me what honesty, forgiveness, and grace look like, for serving Jesus Christ. Your example spurs me to follow Him more.

LYNN AND FLORIN, my sister and brother-in-law—and all my nephews: JONATHAN, STEPHEN, CALEB, AND JOSHUA—what joy you bring to our hearts! Thank you for the love you spread, the lives you live, the hope you have.

JANELLE, my sister, as well—thank you for your caring, giving heart, for the laughs and stories, for the joy you bring to life. You are a true sister and friend!

BOBBY DAVIS—you are an incredibly gifted writer, yet you serve with humility and grace. What a privilege it's been to learn under you! Because of you, I've dared to write.

MOLLIE AND HAL STEENSON, SHELLEY AND J. D. QUINN—thank you for living what you preach, for walking in integrity and compassion, for encouraging and praying for me on this journey. What a blessing it's been to count you as friends and mentors! Because of you all, I've been able to write.

ELDER BILL KNOTT—thank you for believing in what God could do through me, for encouraging Greg and me to grow in Jesus, for being our friend and mentor. Because of you, I've kept on writing.

FOREWORD

I've known Jill Morikone for many years and have always appreciated her speaking and writing abilities. As this book beautifully illustrates, she's immensely skilled at using everyday events to bring out strong spiritual points that both encourage and challenge us.

From her very first chapter, Jill reaches out, grabs our attention, and holds us as she moves from brokenness to forgiveness to a transformed life by the end of the book. As she shares her personal experiences, we suddenly realize that she's being totally transparent, opening her heart to let us look right in! With that level of honesty, it isn't long before we realize that her struggles are the same ones we face each day. Both her victories and defeats inspire us to keep pressing forward! I can truly say that my heart was lifted as I read *HeartLift: Experiencing God's Freedom.*

MOLLIE STEENSON
VICE PRESIDENT
THREE ANGELS BROADCASTING NETWORK

CONTENTS

PART 1

Brokenness

Chapter 1

A HEART THAT'S *BROKEN*

The LORD builds up Jerusalem; He gathers together the outcasts of Israel. He heals the brokenhearted and binds up their wounds.

—PSALM 147:2, 3

I was a young teacher, fresh out of college. Innocent. Naive.

She was a beautiful girl, an upperclassman in academy, gorgeous hair; even, white teeth; perfect complexion; rosy cheeks; a sensitive, caring heart. I'll call her Megan.

She mingled and talked with the other kids, yet somehow she always struck me as a bit lonely, as if she were on the outside, looking in, longing to be part of the action.

Were the other kids ignoring her? Or was she pulling back from them? I couldn't really tell.

Caught up in the whirlwind of teaching for the first time, I didn't draw her out a lot. I'd say, "Hi," as we passed in the halls, but I rarely took the time to sit down and simply talk, to see how she was *really* doing inside, to ask about her heart.

Months passed, and the school took the students on a weekend retreat. I'll never forget that weekend. Megan came to me and asked if we could talk.

"Of course." I smiled as we sat down.

She was wearing a long-sleeved shirt. (I hadn't noticed that she always wore long-sleeved shirts, sweaters, or sweatshirts.)

I caught my breath as I saw the pain in her eyes. *Has it always been there?* I wondered.

"What's on your heart, Megan?"

She turned her head away. "I want to show you something, Miss Jill," she said softly.

I waited, scarcely daring to breathe. *What's going on here?*

She pushed up her long-sleeved shirt, clear to her upper arm. I couldn't see her face. It was still turned away.

I glanced down at her arm. Deep, scarred lines of dried blood crisscrossed her pale skin. Tears filled my eyes. *She's been cutting! Why haven't I seen the signs?*

"Oh, Megan," I breathed.

She shook her head and turned her arm so I could see a little clearer. Suddenly, I noticed they weren't just random slashes in her tender skin. Some of them were, yes. But across her forearm, written with her own blood, she'd cut herself to spell one word—*Help.*

THE PAIN

Even though it's been well over a decade, I can still close my eyes and see the word *Help* etched in blood across her skin. *How long has she been seeking and pleading for help? How many days, weeks, and months have I been too busy to see the pain in this beautiful girl, so desperate for someone to notice?*

Our world is full of people like Megan: women lost and lonely, broken and beaten, hurting and helpless. I'm not talking about physical pain, although many women suffer from that. I'm talking specifically about emotional pain—to my sisters who can't seem to find the face of Jesus, who feel scared and alone, who wander about in darkness, desperately searching for a way out. Or maybe it's baggage they're longing to shed but don't know how; unspoken hurts that need to be forgiven, bottled up bitterness that must be released, a longing to be loved hidden in broken relationships.

Our Father hurts *with* you. He *sees* your pain; He *understands* your weaknesses; He's *eager* to bring help, hope, and healing. After all, He's the God who "heals the brokenhearted and binds up their wounds" (Psalm 147:3).

A couple of months ago, we had a special prayer for one of the women in our congregation. She's a precious woman of God, and although she's lived in constant physical pain, her countenance has always radiated peace, joy, and contentment. Whenever I've asked how she was doing, she's always smiled and said, "I'm doing well, praise God." Even when her pain has been almost overwhelming, she's still smiled, remained cheerful, and spoken encouraging words. However, I knew that chronic pain is debilitating. Eventually, it begins to affect a person's attitude and spiritual walk with Jesus. So I began to pray earnestly for our sister—not just for physical healing, but for the strength and grace to endure.

On this particular Sabbath, we met in the pastor's office to pray. And before we did that, several people shared Scripture verses from their hearts. When my husband Greg's turn came, he repeated the verse I've quoted at the beginning of this chapter. How the Lord could heal the brokenhearted, how He longed to heal that woman's painful wounds. Instead of stopping there, Greg continued reading the next verse, where the psalmist says, "He [God] counts the number of the stars; He calls them all by name" (verse 4). How incredible is that? Our God is so big that He's named all the stars, even though scientists tell us they're innumerable! Yet the same God who holds up the galaxies and names the countless stars, stoops to this little earth, to a little church on this earth, to a small office in that church, even to the heart of my sister, and lovingly whispers, *"I see your pain, My daughter. I see your wounds. I love you with 'an everlasting love' (Jeremiah 31:3). I'll pour My healing and grace into your life."* And that's what we prayed for. Physical healing, yes, if that was God's will. But, most of all, we pleaded for His grace to be made sufficient in her time of weakness (2 Corinthians 12:9), for comfort and peace during this journey (John 14:27), and for continued joy in the midst of her physical suffering.

The beautiful part about this story is that the Lord truly did hear this woman's heart cry and relieved her physical suffering. Shortly after our prayer session, her pain began to diminish and soon disappeared entirely. Praise His name!

THE MASK VERSUS GOD'S WORD

Years ago, on a typical Sabbath morning in church, my older sister and I sat side by side, legs dangling from the pew. Our hair was tied up in colored ribbons, curls cascading down our shoulders, courtesy of an awful night on those pink sponge rollers! Faces scrubbed and shining. Hearts? Not so much.

As the prelude played, people passed by and smiled. Sometimes, they'd stop and ask, "And how are the Penney angels doing today?" (Penney was our maiden name.)

"Oh, we're doing well. Happy Sabbath," we would answer and smile sweetly. However, the moment they turned away, my sister would vigorously jab an elbow into my ribs. (Or did I start it? We're still working on that one.)

Our private elbow war would continue until the next person would stop and talk. Then, our cherubic smiles would reappear, and we'd sweetly answer their questions.

Hypocritical? Absolutely. Even as I think back on those days, I smile at such childish behavior. But, honestly, do we ever really grow up? Whether we're brand-new Christians, or whether we've been in church for years but are still babes in Christ, the mask of good Christianity is easy to slip on.

I ought to know. I wore it for years.

I grew up thinking my struggle was a solitary one. So many of the men and women I admired in the church seemed to really have it all together. They were always happy, always cheerful, always serving Jesus and saying the right things.

Then, as I grew older, people began to say those same things about me. "Oh, Jill, you really follow Jesus. You're always smiling, always seeking to minister." The truth was that many days I *did* walk right beside my Jesus— but not every day. Some days, I'd begin by spending time in His Word and praying. I'd feel connected to Jesus, but then bitterness or self-pity would suddenly rear its ugly head. Sometimes the accusing voice of Satan would whisper, "Who do you think you are, pretending to serve Jesus like this? Don't you know you're really a nobody?" And I would tremble with fear. I would fall to my knees, seeking my Father's face, only to find that my prayers seemed to hit the ceiling and bounce back.

What had happened? Hadn't the day begun with Jesus? Why didn't my feelings match my faith? If only I could *know* that God heard my prayers and was with me, all would be well. However, on those days when I couldn't *feel* His presence, I always doubted myself. On those days, I wore the mask I'd seen modeled for me during all my growing-up years—the mask of good Christianity.

I'm sure you've seen, or even experienced, this mask. Maybe you can't forgive someone who has deeply hurt you, and the resentment is simmering just beneath the surface. Yet you smile in church and pretend everything is fine, even while you tighten the lid on the tumult you feel inside.

Or, no matter how hard you pray, maybe you've never experienced peace in Jesus, never had assurance of your salvation. Yet you lead out in church— maybe even give Bible studies.

Perhaps you've just yelled at your kids, and then the doorbell rang and you greeted the person with, "Oh, it's so good to see you again! Yes, we're all doing well. Won't you come in and have something to drink?" As you invite him or her in, you glance at your kids. Yes, they're learning well how to model "good Christianity," how to wear the mask.

As I was praying over this problem in my life, I suddenly stumbled upon (or rather, God in His mercy revealed) the answer to my problem with my feelings. I discovered the absolute power of the Word of God, the promises we can claim, and how our God can actually change our feelings to match our faith in His Word! As I began to experience God's victory more and more frequently in my life, my joy grew. This was incredible; this was what I'd been searching for! God was truly able to keep me from falling, and to present me "faultless before the presence of His glory with exceeding joy" (Jude 24).

THE JOURNEY

I don't know where you are in your walk with Jesus, my sister. Perhaps you're cowering in the corner, afraid to come to Him. If so, He says, "The one who comes to Me I will by no means cast out" (John 6:37).

Maybe you're angry at someone who's hurt you, and you can't release that bitterness. He promises that He has come "to preach deliverance to the captives, . . . to set at liberty them that are bruised" (Luke 4:18, KJV).

Maybe you're terrified of some diagnosis, disaster, or difficulty. He longs to take away your fear and fill you with His peace (John 14:27; 1 John 4:18).

No matter what your pain, problem, or issue, Jesus has a solution. He has a beautiful plan for your life, a plan to prosper you and not to harm you, a plan to "give you a future and a hope" (Jeremiah 29:11). He so desires you to have an abundant life (John 10:10)! Whatever your impurity, He can cleanse it (1 John 1:9). Whatever your sorrow, He'll turn it into joy (John 16:20). Whatever your weakness, He'll give you strength (2 Corinthians 12:9).

You don't have to live in pain, defeated and downcast. Neither do you have to wear that mask forever.

You can be set free! And whomever Jesus sets free, is free indeed (John 8:36)!

PART 2

Forgiveness

Chapter 2

A HEART THAT *ACCEPTS* *GOD'S FORGIVENESS*

Behold what manner of love the Father has bestowed on us, that we should be called the children of God!

—1 JOHN 3:1

She was just a little thing. In fact, when the half-starved gray tabby adopted us, she was barely out of kittenhood. We named her Pebbles, and she grew to love our yard—sleeping in the flower beds; rolling on her back in our gravel driveway; pouncing on unsuspecting bugs, beetles, or birds.

Her longer expeditions came when we walked. She would trot alongside us for a while and then take refuge beside the road to wait for our return trip. We never had to call her; she always emerged from the weeds when we walked past. Back arched, tail up and waving proudly, she'd escort us home.

Pebbles had been with us for about four years when the unthinkable happened—she disappeared. Greg and I had traveled for 3ABN; and upon our return, we discovered she'd been missing for several days. As dusk descended, we hurried into the field, calling and pausing, straining our ears for the slightest sound.

Pebbles always came home. What had happened to her? Maybe she'd been caught by one of the owls or hawks that lived near us. Maybe an extra-hungry coyote had helped himself to an easy meal. She'd never been a good fighter.

I turned to Greg as we trudged home wearily. "Do you think she's hurt or needs us? Do you think she's dead?"

Greg reached for my hand. "I don't know, Jilly. Only God knows right now, but we can trust Him with her life."

He was right, of course. But I didn't want to think about that right then. I just wanted her home.

The next morning around 5:00 A.M., we ran to the front porch and flipped on the light. No sign of her anywhere. *How could a little stray tabby cat have wrapped herself so completely around my heart?* I wondered.

Mechanically, I made our breakfast and forced a few bites down my tight throat. Just as the sun came up, Greg left for work, and I pulled on a pair of his old jeans and an old coat. Breathing a prayer, I stretched my leg over the barbed wire fence across the lane, and almost immediately the thicket forced me to my hands and knees.

I forged ahead, dodging deer droppings and poison ivy, yanking my coat off of a thornbush. Always stopping, always calling, but hearing no *meow*.

After an hour, I struggled back to our gravel road and turned up a field. Walking the tree line, I called once more, and heard the faintest *meow*.

Am I hearing things?

I stopped and called again. *Meow.* It was louder this time. I crashed into the trees. *Pebby, I'm coming for you! I love you!*

Her meows strengthened as I got closer. Then, suddenly, I saw her. Back arched, tail waving proudly. She rubbed against me and purred. And me—I sat down and cried! She was just a little thing. Why hadn't she come home? Maybe she'd been lost. Maybe the way home looked too far. Maybe she was too tired to walk anymore.

Knowing she disliked being carried, I started walking for home, hoping she'd keep pace with me. Instead, she just sat and looked at me, so I bent down, picked her up, and held her close against my chest. She didn't struggle. She had no fight left. She just knew I loved her, and she wanted to go home.

Across the field we went, a dirty, scratched-up woman and a little worn-out cat. Both content and filled with joy. As I carried her, my mind traveled to the many times my Father, the Shepherd, had looked for me and called me; of all the times He'd braved the brambles and thickets for me; of the miles He'd walked pursuing me.

Sometimes, I think I purposefully hid. I heard His voice calling, yet was afraid—afraid of a holy God seeing my sin-polluted heart. Other times I got lost and turned around—and just couldn't seem to find my way back home.

Still other times, I was so worn out by the fight that I didn't think I could take another step. Those were the times He had bent down, gently picked me up, and carried me home close against His chest, close to His heart. How thankful I was that He had cared enough to search, that He hadn't given up, that He'd *loved* me!

Pebbles and I crossed the road into our yard. She hadn't stirred a muscle. We walked around to the garage, and I knelt down and gently placed the exhausted kitty on the ground. "It's OK, Pebbles," I whispered. "You're home."

COMING TO JESUS

Do you feel far from God? Have you heard His voice calling for you, yet were afraid to come to Him? Afraid He'd see the filth covering you? Or perhaps, you've asked for forgiveness again and again but don't feel forgiven. You don't feel worthy, don't truly feel like you're a daughter of the King.

I know. I've been there.

For years, I felt like I couldn't come back to God right away every time I slipped into sin. I'd think, *If I stay away for a while and try to be good, then maybe God will be more willing to accept me. Maybe, I can do some sort of penance.* Coming immediately to God asking for forgiveness just seemed too cheap, too easy. Surely, it had to be harder!

The truth is this: There's nothing *easy* about forgiveness! Forgiveness of sin comes at a high price—too high, in fact, for you or me ever to pay. We can never be *good enough,* for "all our righteousness are like filthy rags" (Isaiah 64:6). The best we can do is *still* tainted with sin. We can never measure up.

Yet, Someone *did* measure up. Someone *did* pay the price—the ultimate price. Someone lived a perfect life and died a perfect death. Someone spilled His blood on Calvary.

Why?

Because He loves us. Because He knew we'd never measure up. Because He wanted to set us free!

This morning, Greg and I woke up at the usual time and began our early morning time with God. How I love that time with God's Word and with my Savior! Just as I was getting into a special promise from my Bible, Greg walked in.

"The weather on my phone says the roads might be slick this morning," he said. "Do you think we got some snow?"

We flipped on the outside floodlights and peeked out through the blinds. Sure enough, a beautiful layer of white covered the brown grass and mud of winter. Snow! As I sit typing this, I glance out our sliding glass door and see the soft, white covering of snow. How it dazzles and sparkles when the sun comes out. How pure. How beautiful.

A pastor once told me that his name for me was, "Pure as the undriven snow." When he said that, I knew it wasn't true. I knew about the smeared mud inside my heart. Oh, how I wanted to be clean, but I didn't know how. I'd asked for forgiveness, but my heart still felt dirty. However, the truth is, my sister, that when we confess and forsake our sins, our Father truly does see us as pure as undriven—untouched—snow! He invites, "Come now, and let us reason together," and promises,

> "Though your sins are like scarlet,
> They shall be as white as snow;
> Though they are red like crimson,
> They shall be as wool" (Isaiah 1:18).

Our Savior knows all about our weaknesses, all about our dirty hearts, all about our sins. Just now, He's searching for you through the brambles and thickets, across the fields of life, calling, "Come home, My daughter. Please come home! For why should you die?" (Ezekiel 18:31).

→ FEELING VERSUS FAITH

You might be saying, "Jill, I want to come home, but He could never forgive me. He could never accept me!" If so, let me tell you something that happened to me recently. I was walking through the church sanctuary after the service. We had enjoyed a powerful sermon, and my heart was blessed. Now, as I passed a certain pew, one of my fellow church members stopped me.

"Jill, I need to talk with you, if you have a minute," she said, so I sat down next to her, and my precious sister shared from her heart. Tears began to flow as she related her pain and the issues she was struggling with. As we got to the root of the issue, she said, "I want to pray, Jill. I want to believe! But how do I know that God truly hears me? I can't *feel* Him. I can't *touch* Him. I don't have any peace! How do I know He will accept me?"

As she spoke, my mind traveled to the many similar struggles I'd had as a new Christian, then to another friend who couldn't feel *forgiven,* and yet another who didn't feel *worthy.* My sister was facing a very real battle! In fact, I believe it's one of Satan's favorite tactics in this war for our hearts and minds.

You see, if he can rob us of our peace and joy in Jesus, if he can take away our assurance of salvation, he strips us of our identity in Christ. We could spend our entire lives caught in his trap, never breaking free from his guilt and condemnation.

However, this is where faith comes in! A statement I recently read says, "When you can't feel God with your feelings, feel Him with your faith." And how can I build my faith, you ask? Spend time in the Word of God (Romans 10:17).

One of the best-known Bible texts on forgiveness is found in 1 John 1:9. As you read it, speak it aloud, for "death and life are in the power of the tongue" (Proverbs 18:21). Personalize the verse, put your name in there! Don't listen to what the devil is throwing at you. Don't let him say you're not good enough or not worthy enough. Jesus died just for you! He gave *everything* just so you could be free.

Say it out loud with me: "If (say your name here) confesses her sins, He is faithful and just to actually forgive her and to cleanse her from all unrighteousness" (1 John 1:9, author's paraphrase).

"But," you say, "I don't feel any different. How can I know for sure that Jesus has forgiven me?"

You can know because God stands behind His Word. You can know because He "is not a man, that He should lie" (Numbers 23:19). You can know because "as far as the east is from the west, so far has He removed our transgressions from us" (Psalm 103:12).

Say out loud, "*My Father* has forgiven me. My Father has *forgiven* me. My Father has forgiven *me.* Thank You, Father, for Your forgiveness. By faith, I'm accepting what Your Word says about me." And you know what, my friend? *The feelings will come!* They always do. Our feelings follow our thoughts; and if our minds choose to believe what God's Word says about us, then our feelings will come into line with our thoughts. It may take a while. It may be an intense battle. But all Heaven is on our side! Our feelings will come to match our faith in His Word.

CONVICTION VERSUS CONDEMNATION

Recently, Greg and I were in Massachusetts visiting my family. We drove into a city and stopped at a cute little restaurant. It wasn't part of a chain, just a little place tucked into a city block, but offered exceptional Thai food. As we waited for our meal, my cell phone rang. Excusing myself, I answered the call. It was a friend from church. Her pain was raw and intense from doing combat with the enemy. She was earnestly seeking God but was troubled by an overwhelming sense of condemnation. "You're not good enough," Satan taunted. "What type of Christian wife and mother are you?"

As she spoke, I was reminded of a truth that my friend Rhonda had shared with me: "Condemnation never comes from Jesus. The Holy Spirit brings conviction of sin, yes; but condemnation always comes from the enemy." This is not only relevant for the hurting woman who had phoned me, but also for me and for struggling women everywhere.

So how can we know the difference? What is conviction from God, and what is condemnation from the enemy? For me, the biggest difference comes from the *spirit* behind the thought. Let me explain. If the thought has anything to do with my worth as a woman of God, then it's condemnation. Satan is good at throwing stuff our way: "Who do you think you are? Getting up to speak? You're nothing but a failure!"

We can rebuke him instantly in the name of Jesus, for our God has called us to speak for Him (Exodus 4:12); He's called us to share Him, even if we are "earthen vessels" (2 Corinthians 4:7); He's called us to show Him to the world (1 Peter 2:9).

However, when God brings conviction, it pierces our hearts—but never in a demeaning, belittling way (Hebrews 4:12). Sometimes, it comes from unrest in my spirit, and I feel uncomfortable about a conversation I just had with someone. If there's unrest, God is trying to show me something. So I pray, "Search me, O God, and know my heart; try me, and know my anxieties" (Psalm 139:23). I ask Him to reveal anything to me that is displeasing to Him (verse 24).

At other times, the Holy Spirit speaks to my heart in a still, small Voice. *"Jill, what you just said wasn't entirely true. My daughters are honest. Go back and tell the truth."*

Notice that if Satan were bringing the same accusation, he would say, "You've never been honest! You're such a failure. Why even try?"

Do you see the difference? Our Father brings conviction; Satan brings discouragement. Our God reveals our sin and already has a solution; the enemy taunts, torments, and offers us no hope. Our Savior deals redemptively; Satan deals destructively. Praise God, we don't have to listen to the lies of the enemy!

I don't know where you are in your journey with Jesus, my sister. Maybe you're still hiding in the woods, listening as Jesus calls you, and cowering as you see Him forge a path to your heart. You may be longing for deliverance but are ashamed and afraid to let Him see your filth. Oh, how He loves you! Even now, He's drawing you with His "everlasting love" (Jeremiah 31:3). He's saying, "The one who comes to Me I will by no means cast out" (John 6:37). Come. Come just now, and find forgiveness and cleansing.

On the other hand, you may have asked again and again for forgiveness, yet still don't feel His acceptance, don't have assurance of your salvation, don't truly feel clean. Just open your heart anew to Him. Accept *by faith* what His Word says about you. Choose to walk in freedom. You are the cleansed, purified bride of the King!

Chapter 3

A HEART THAT
FORGIVES OTHERS

Bearing with one another, and forgiving one another, if anyone has a complaint against another; even as Christ forgave you, so you also must do.
—COLOSSIANS 3:13

The room had already grown a bit stuffy. It always did. The women crowded in—some merely to break up the monotony of their day, but others were eager to hear the Word of God. They sat four across on the large desk, legs dangling midair. A few lucky ones got one of the chairs in the room. Others stood along the cement-block walls or sat cross-legged on the floor, orange crocs contrasting with their blue jail uniforms.

I stood along the wall, squeezed between the desk and one of the chairs. One of our sisters from church was leading the study that day, and she opened with some familiar Bible texts about the love of God, His forgiveness, and the forgiveness promises we can claim.

I glanced around the circle. Most of the women were into the study, their Bibles open as they followed along. A few whispered and giggled in the corner.

Suddenly, the leader closed her Bible and began sharing from her heart. She began to reveal how she struggled with forgiveness—both toward her father, who was in prison for abusing her and her siblings, and toward herself, for not reporting his abuse sooner.

Instantly, the atmosphere changed. The whispers ceased, and thirteen pairs of eyes were riveted on her as she shared her pain, heartache, and the hope she has in Jesus. Some leaned forward in their seats, others looked at the floor and wept softly, yet all of them could identify in some way.

Maybe they hadn't been molested as kids, but they all struggled with guilt.

One woman cried as she shared the guilt she carried for killing another woman in a car accident. Another carried bitterness against a family member whom she didn't trust around her kids, yet there she was in jail, unable to protect them. Still another was there on drug charges but unable to forgive her mom for turning her in to the authorities.

Different issues, different problems; but all the women faced the issue of forgiveness. Could they be forgiven for what they had done? And, if they could, what about the others involved? Could they forgive those who had hurt them the most?

UNWILLING TO FORGIVE

I don't know what hurt or pain you've faced in your life, what bitterness is eating away at your heart. Maybe you've endured abuse like my friend who led the study group. Maybe you've been gossiped about or maligned. Maybe you're carrying a grudge against one of your friends in church—or even against your husband.

We've all known people who have hurt us in some way or another. Sometimes it's an accident or simply a matter of miscommunication. But at other times it's purposeful, spiteful, and vengeful. What do we do then? How can we forgive when the pain is so deep? And doesn't forgiving these people let them off the hook?

I believe forgiveness has more to do with us—with our own personal walk with Jesus—than it does with anybody else. We can't change the other person. Nor can we manufacture forgiveness ourselves. But we can choose to forgive God's way. We can choose to walk His path.

BEGIN BY TRUSTING GOD

First, we need to ask ourselves several questions: Do I trust God enough to truly work everything out for good in the end (Romans 8:28)? Do I trust Him to bring justice and vengeance Himself—instead of taking on that task myself (Romans 12:19)? Do I trust His Word enough to leave the results with Him?

God never intended any of the pain and misery in this world. His original plan was perfection—perfect peace, perfect love, and perfect harmony between us and God, each other, and nature. God rules with love and truth; Satan rules with force and deception. Yet, in the midst of all this suffering, do we trust that our God can bring beauty from ashes (Isaiah 61:3), joy after tears (Psalm 30:5), and healing after pain? Can we trust Him to work out His beautiful plan for our lives—a plan to prosper us and not harm us, a plan to give us a hope and a future (Jeremiah 29:11)?

Maybe you've heard Babbie Mason's beautiful song "Trust His Heart." It's one of my favorites when I'm struggling with something. Yes, there are problems in this world. Yes, we can't always understand. But our God *never* makes a mistake! When we don't *understand* what's happening, when we can't *see* the future, we can still trust His heart.

God loves you, my sister. Trust Him!

SURRENDER

I believe surrender is closely linked with trust. If I trust God, I'll be willing to surrender to Him. On the other hand, I cannot truly surrender unless I trust.

My sister has three little men in her home. Right now they're six, four, and one and a half years old, and her fourth child is due in a few weeks. Being a mom to three active boys is a full-time job. It can be intense.

She lives in North Carolina, and as we spoke on the phone recently about snack time, loose teeth, and birthday parties, she told me a story. It happened last summer as one of those violent storms came through, you know the ones with all the lightning and thunder, wind and rain, hail and potential tornadoes. They don't have a full basement, but they do have a crawl space, so as the storm came through that night, her guys slept peacefully while she stayed up listening to the weather scanner wondering if they should take shelter.

Then it came. *Beep. Beep. Beep. Beep.* "The National Weather Service in . . ."

A tornado had been spotted. "Seek shelter immediately!"

She sprang to her feet and ran to the boys' bedroom. Grabbing one sleeping son, she hurried with him under the house, laying him on a sleeping bag she'd already put there in anticipation. Then she dashed upstairs, picked up the next warm, peaceful son, and rushed back to the crawl space. The process was repeated until all had safely taken shelter. And the amazing part was that none of the boys woke up until sometime later! They slept peacefully through the violent storm, through the flight to shelter.

Do you realize that we can have that same experience? The same peace regardless of who has hurt us or what has been done against us? If we truly surrender, we can rest with a peaceful heart, trusting in our heavenly Father to work out all things well in behalf of His children!

Maybe someone is talking about you behind your back and the pain is intense. Can you trust those comments to Him? Can you trust His Word that every tongue that rises against you will be condemned at the judgment (Isaiah 54:17)? Can you trust that He is still in control and that you can walk humbly with God, trusting Him to take care of your reputation?

Or maybe it's bigger than that. Maybe someone killed your son while driving drunk, and your rage and desire for revenge is overwhelming.

God didn't cause that accident to happen. Can you still trust Him in the midst of it all? Can you accept that He can still give peace, that He can still grant forgiveness, that He can still give you love?

As I write these words, my own heart is trembling. You see, I've never been tested to that extent. Greg and I don't have children, and I've never lost a close relative in a situation like that. We've faced death in our family before—and death is painful—but we've never been confronted with something so sinister, so evil. It seems much harder to forgive, because the offender has a face!

What would I do? I truly don't know. But I *do* know this: I trust my Father. I love my Savior. And, as I'm faced with the small stuff every day, the easier-to-forgive stuff, I'm choosing to surrender, choosing to ask for His forgiveness because I can't manufacture it myself, choosing to deal with the pain His way.

RECOGNIZE THAT FORGIVENESS ISN'T OPTIONAL FOR A CHRISTIAN

Oh, we can wrestle with forgiveness, dodge it, turn our backs to it, but the need for forgiveness is still there, staring us in the face.

In my mind's eye, I see a picture of Someone who didn't dodge or turn His back. Someone who offered forgiveness freely—even before it was asked of Him. I see His hands stretched out upon that rough wood, the long spikes being driven into His tender flesh, and hear those words uttered from pale, quivering lips—and a heart of love: "Father, forgive them, for they do not know what they do" (Luke 23:34).

Even as the Son of God was being killed, He didn't offer forgiveness through clenched teeth. He didn't say, "I know you don't deserve it, but I'm choosing to forgive you, you hard-hearted rebels!" He knew they weren't even ready to ask forgiveness of Him. Instead, He freely asked forgiveness of His Father on their behalf. That's a heart that thinks of others before Himself. What an example! What sacrifice! What love!

Earlier, during the Sermon on the Mount, Jesus said, "If you forgive men their trespasses, your heavenly Father will also forgive you. But if you do not forgive men their trespasses, neither will your Father forgive your trespasses" (Matthew 6:14, 15). It's a principle of God's kingdom! How can He forgive us when we're hanging on to a grudge, when we're refusing to forgive someone else? The truth is God isn't being unfair or unjust here. He is just pointing out the obvious connection. How can He truly work in our lives when we won't allow Him in? When we won't give Him access to our entire hearts? When we hold on to feelings of revenge and bitterness?

FINALLY, ASK GOD FOR HIS FORGIVENESS

Perhaps your pain and resentment are bottled up deep inside you. Our Father hurts with you. He knows you can't give up your bitterness.

Go to Him now! Tell Him what He already knows. Ask Him to do a work in your heart and to uproot what you can't pull out yourself. Give Him permission to come in and take out your heart of stone and give you a heart of flesh (Ezekiel 36:26, 27). Surrender, and then go free! Trust Him to complete the work He's begun in your life (Philippians 1:6).

You don't have to take Satan's guilt and shame. You can stand up as God's daughter—purified before Him. By faith, you can accept His forgiveness and allow Him to take the bitterness out of your heart. Just let Him in.

Chapter 4

A HEART THAT'S *BITTER*

Let all bitterness, wrath, anger, clamor, and evil speaking be put away from you, with all malice. And be kind to one another, tenderhearted, forgiving one another, even as God in Christ forgave you.
—EPHESIANS 4:31, 32

From the beginning, I felt uncertain, a bit wary, never quite free to be me. A friend I'll call Janie was gifted in many areas. Because she was fairly forceful in sharing her opinions, ours was definitely a tightrope relationship.

As I stepped into a room one day, I heard unfamiliar voices and one I recognized. She had her back to me and was surrounded by a crowd, so I hesitated just an instant, and that's when the talk shifted.

I froze in place as I realized Janie was talking about me. Words poured forth—critical words, belittling words, cutting words. Stung, I stood rooted to the spot, unable to tear myself away. After what seemed like an eternity, but more likely just a few seconds, I turned and slipped away.

That day, our relationship took a nosedive. Oh, I never told Janie what I'd overheard, and neither did I tell anyone else. Like any "good Christian," I smugly thought I was handling the matter well. After all, I wasn't gossiping about her, and I still treated her politely. However, I was bottling up a simmering resentment.

Several months passed. Deliberately ignoring and suppressing the turmoil inside, I naively thought all was well between Jesus and me. Then one day, as I washed dishes, I began memorizing a new Bible text: "Pursue peace with all people, and holiness, without which no one will see the Lord," I repeated as I scrubbed a plate (Hebrews 12:14). I rejoiced in the fact that, to the best of my knowledge, my heart was right with Jesus and with my fellow church members. (My resentment was buried so deeply that I couldn't sense it!)

Then came a sudden jolt as my eyes scanned the next verse: "Looking carefully lest anyone fall short of the grace of God; lest any root of bitterness springing up cause trouble, and by this many become defiled" (verse 15).

Instantly, the Holy Spirit brought conviction! *"Jill, you've got bitterness bottled up in your heart. This bitterness is not only affecting you, it will spread to affect your marriage, your friends, and your ministry."*

How earnestly I sought forgiveness for the resentment boiling inside me. However, buried bitterness doesn't fade away easily. Every time I saw Janie, I felt my chest tighten, and I soon realized that a root of bitterness still controlled me.

Each day I asked God to remove it, but still it lurked, deep in the recesses of my heart. How could I be set free?

BITTERNESS VERSUS LOVE

The effects of bitterness are widespread. How often do we see it rear its ugly head as petty jealousies and cherished grudges divide both churches and homes? Has it taken root in your home? Are you bitter or resentful against your husband for something he said, a decision he's made, or a stand he's taken? Or maybe you're nursing bitterness against a parent or a sibling.

The Bible says that a single root of bitterness can affect many, and God certainly revealed that fact to me that day as I washed dishes (verse 15). He showed me that my bitterness would soon spread to infect others. What I thought was my private, carefully coddled sin was already reaching its tentacles toward the people whom I loved the most.

Greg and I planted an herb garden along the south side of our garage. It gets direct sunlight all day, and most of the herbs seem to flourish there. Then, several years ago, I was delighted when a friend gave me some of her extra herbs, and among them were a few mint plants. Crushing a leaf, I inhaled the fragrant aroma. *Ah, this will be nice among my other herbs!* (I'm sure that if you're a gardener, you're already smiling to yourself. You know how this story ends!)

That first year the mint filled in the holes nicely, and I was pleased with the result. However, the second summer, I noticed that it had begun to take over my garden. My basil was boxed in, my oregano was overrun, and my cilantro was crowded. I yanked and pulled on the mint, but it just continued to proliferate. It grew into the lawn and smelled nice when Greg mowed, but that wasn't the point. I just couldn't seem to get it under control!

By the third year, I was desperate; at the end of the summer, we pulled up all the plants—the good and the bad—used weed killer liberally, and let the garden rest. When I replanted my herb garden, you can be sure I did not include mint!

How our heavenly Father's heart must break as He sees His sons and daughters holding on to grudges, cherishing bitterness, spurning His healing and reconciliation.

During Jesus' last meal with His disciples before His crucifixion, He spoke to them about this. After He demonstrated love and humility in action by washing their feet, He shared from His heart: "A new commandment I give to you, that you love one another; as I have loved you, that you also love one another" (John 13:34).

He knew they were striving for supremacy. He understood they weren't all converted. He saw into their hearts and saw their self-centeredness, their grudges, and their bitterness. Then He gave this litmus test for discipleship: "By this all will know that you are My disciples, if you have love for one another" (verse 35).

As I look into my own heart, the Holy Spirit asks me that question anew: *"Jill, do you have love for your brothers and sisters?"* Oh, it's easy to love those who love us in return; it's simple to be kind to those who treat us kindly; it's painless to reach out to those without prickles. The real test comes when the loving costs us something, when it's uncomfortable, when it hurts.

Some time ago, I received a letter from a woman who decided to address some issues she saw in my life. Some of her observations were accurate, and some probably weren't; but at first, all I could feel was the sting of her words. I tried to forgive her, but I knew that a root of bitterness was still troubling my heart.

Early one morning, as I spent time with my Savior, I began to read Romans 15. First, Paul instructs believers to have unity among themselves. Then he says, "Therefore receive one another, just as Christ also received us, to the glory of God" (Romans 15:7).

Once again, the Holy Spirit spoke to my heart. *"Jill, I've accepted you. I've forgiven you. But I have also accepted your sister—you know, the woman toward whom you feel bitterness."*

I began to squirm. This was hitting a little too close to home! *"Since I've accepted her as My daughter, don't you think you could accept her as your sister?"* So I repented. I asked God to grant me His love and forgiveness for her. I prayed for her and, a few days later, God released my bitterness.

A few months later, I received another letter from the same woman, apologizing for the spirit in which she'd written her previous letter. God did it! I never had to go to her about it. He impressed on her heart where she was wrong—just as He'd showed me my own bitterness.

The way I see it, the issue of loving each other as brothers and sisters comes down to this: Christ has forgiven me, loved me, and accepted me. Therefore, I am to accept my sister and my brother. It's that simple. We receive each other because Christ has received us. We love because "He first loved us" (1 John 4:19). We forgive because He has forgiven us. "Freely you have received, freely give" (Matthew 10:8).

GOD'S SOLUTION

"But, what if my bitterness has been bottled up for years?" you ask. "I don't know how to eradicate it! I've been asking God for freedom, but I just can't break free."

I understand. Remember my bitterness toward Janie that I mentioned earlier in this chapter? How I was asking God to remove my bitterness, but it wouldn't go away? Well, let me tell you what finally happened.

In a final act of desperation, I decided to pray for Janie. Not just a quick, easy prayer but a painful prayer—one that would cost me something. Each day I pleaded with God for Janie, for her home and her marriage, for her health and her job, for her children and her family. I pleaded for God to shower her with financial and spiritual blessings, for Him to use her in His service, for Him to stand her up to be all He's called her to be as God's daughter.

Day one—no change.

Day two—the same.

Day three—ditto.

Then, on about day four or five, God transformed my heart. I have no idea how He did it, I just know He did. Gone was the bitterness, the desire for revenge, that sick feeling in the pit of my stomach at the mere mention of her name. Jesus had won! Prayer, coupled with surrender, made the difference for me.

In the beginning when you pray with surrender, your prayer will probably feel fake. I know it did for me. I was still bitter—still angry with Janie. So why was I pleading with God to bless her? I would rather have asked Him to bring some sort of punishment to her! But that is not how forgiveness works. Jesus says to "love your enemies, bless those who curse you, do good to those who hate you, and pray for those who spitefully use you and persecute you" (Matthew 5:44).

How painful is that?

At first glance, it seems impossible, but with God *nothing* is impossible (Luke 1:37). God delights in taking our impossible attitudes and transforming them. He's overjoyed to give us the grace we need to overcome; He's so pleased when we call on Him for help.

One of my friends is in the middle of this battle right now. She's feeling hurt. She has been betrayed. She has bottled up bitterness. However, in spite of her feelings, she's choosing to trust, choosing to surrender, choosing to pray. Is her battle over yet? Far from it. In fact, she's in the hottest part of the battle right now. But I know that Jesus will give her the victory. We're claiming this promise by faith: "If the Son makes you free, you shall be free indeed" (John 8:36).

FORGIVENESS VERSUS TRUST

I don't want to close this chapter without touching on an important issue—trust. Recently, a reader e-mailed me with a question after reading my story of how the Lord had removed my bitterness toward Janie. She understood that God had given me His forgiveness for her, but she wanted to know about my current relationship with her. Specifically, she asked if I could bring myself to trust Janie again. Had God restored our relationship to that extent?

God gave me His forgiveness for Janie; and yes, we're able to pray together and share together. But does that mean I can trust her?

I believe that trust is earned. And when it is broken, it isn't automatically restored. It takes time for that person to demonstrate trustworthiness again.

For instance, if people commit crimes and are sent to prison, will they be repeat offenders after they've served their time? The answer is Yes—and No. If they haven't repented and allowed Jesus to transform them, then Yes, they might commit that crime again. However, if they've been truly converted, if Jesus has transformed their hearts by the renewing of their minds, then No, they won't break that law again.

How do we know? Only with time and the slow rebuilding of trust.

Once we've forgiven them, once God has released the bitterness from our hearts, we allow Him to heal our relationships—in His time.

Continue watching: Has the person changed? Is he or she trustworthy again? If you feel you can't trust him or her yet, it's OK; just continue to love the person. Keep right on praying for him or her. Do things with him or her; just don't share intimate, personal things from your own heart yet. God will show you when—and if—that should take place.

I don't know where your heart is in your own battle with forgiveness, but I urge you to come to our Father just now. Ask Him for His forgiveness, and then pray. Pray earnestly. Pray perseveringly. Pray untiringly!

Pray for God's blessings to be abundantly poured out on the person who has hurt you. Pray for Him to bless that person—financially, with health, and with spiritual blessings in Christ Jesus. As you pray, God is at work, transforming your own heart and life.

What a testament to the power of the gospel—that Jesus will take any of us, that He can enable us to walk in love and forgiveness with each other, that He longs to pour out His power into simple jars of clay (2 Corinthians 4:6, 7). Praise His name!

PART 3

Fear

Chapter 5

A HEART THAT'S *AFRAID*

There is no fear in love; but perfect love casts out fear.
—1 JOHN 4:18

Catch me, Daddy. Catch me!" It's a scene that's been played over and over for generations. Little Sarah stands at the top of the slide or the stairs or the tree house. It doesn't matter *where*. It makes no difference *who*. Neither is *why* an issue. It's simple, unconditional trust—perfect love played out, over and over.

Little chubby arms are held out. Little legs push off, and the child takes the great plunge into open space, knowing there is safety, there is love, there is a great big daddy ready to catch her before she hits the ground. There's no question, no doubt in that little mind. *Daddy can do anything. Daddy loves me, and he won't let me get hurt. Of course, Daddy can catch me!*

Sometimes that innocence is snatched away all at once, but more often, it gradually dissipates. Little minds grow up, little hearts change, and life's experiences begin to mold little Sarah. Satan begins to tell Sarah lies about herself, about others, and about her heavenly Father. Fear's dark tentacles begin to reach into Sarah's life, and unconditional love and trust are slowly squelched.

By the time I reached adulthood, fear had plowed a deep rut in my mind. It became almost natural—second nature—for me to respond with fear or worry. Part of it came from the lies that Satan force-fed me, part of it from environmental influences, and another part from my refusal to take every thought captive to Jesus Christ as I grew up. But whatever the reason, by the time I was twenty, fear dictated much of my behavior, influenced my decisions, and ruled my life.

Thank God, however, Jesus could set me free! He came to set the captives free, to preach liberty to those who are bound (Luke 4:18). He longed to break the chains that bound me to my fears. But before we look at Jesus' deliverance, let's consider the types of fears that Satan enslaves us with.

FEARS ABOUT GOD

They were the envy of the neighborhood, the talk of the town (if there had been one). She was the most beautiful woman to walk this earth—perfect in face, in form, and in heart. Her husband was tall, strong, and handsome—a strong leader, yet tender; firmly devoted to God, yet compassionate; hardworking, yet swift to encourage others.

Their marriage was never marred by a critical spirit or even so much as a single harsh word. Perfect harmony existed between the two and between them and their Maker—their God. They had steady employment, a beautiful home, and numerous activities and playmates. Most important, they enjoyed unbroken, unceasing communion with their King.

Into Adam and Eve's perfect world came Satan the deceiver. He was the first to tell lies about God, lies that Eve fell for. That evening, when God came to visit them as He'd done every evening since they were created, the Bible tells us that "Adam and his wife hid themselves from the presence of the LORD God" (Genesis 3:8).

Why did they hide? They had always loved talking with God! Genesis 3:10 tells us Adam's answer: "I heard Your voice in the garden, and I was afraid . . . and I hid myself."

God wasn't separating Himself from them. He was walking in the Garden, looking for them. He even called for them. He didn't turn His back on them. The truth is simply that sin brings fear and guilt. Their sin separated them from Jesus.

Almost immediately, they began to believe the devil's lies about God. When God asked Adam why he had eaten of the fruit, he instantly blamed his wife—and God! "You gave me this woman. It's Your fault that I'm in this mess!" (see verse 12). Eve, in turn, didn't accept the blame but turned it toward the serpent.

Throughout earth's history—beginning with the Garden of Eden—Satan has misrepresented the character of God. He still constantly feeds us lies: God is a stern, unforgiving ruler; God causes evil and suffering; God is the author of all the misery we see in this world.

Why would our enemy do this? Because he wants to make us *fear* God, to serve Him out of fear instead of love. He wants to rob us of our joy and victory in Jesus, to cause us to live constantly in fear.

If he can prevent us from believing that we're worthy enough to be forgiven, then he has succeeded in keeping us in bondage. We could spend our entire lives struggling but never having peace and assurance in Jesus. We could waste years of our lives standing terrified at the top of the slide, afraid to trust God and jump.

How many times have you heard Satan's lies?

"If you really choose to follow Jesus, He'll bring you into a trial of some sort that will practically finish you—for your own character growth, of course."

Or what about this one: "There must have been some sin in their lives. That's why they're dealing with cancer. I always knew they should have eaten a better diet."

Or even this one: "If God is all powerful, why didn't He stop that little girl from being abused? Does that mean He caused it?"

You see how insidious Satan is? Always twisting the truth, always insinuating that God *doesn't* really love us, that He doesn't really have our best interests at heart, that He is untrustworthy.

Fear—it began with sin and Satan, and he spreads it to a captive and willing audience.

But fears about God are not the only ones he spreads. Let's look at some others.

OTHER FEARS

The room was small and sterile, cold and uninviting. We waited, the three of us, in a sort of breathless silence. What was the use of small talk? We'd already said everything, hoped everything, and prayed everything. Now, only the doctor's verdict remained unstated.

My mom sat on the doctor's exam table; my dad leaned against the wall nearby, arms folded across his chest. Too nervous to sit, I took my stance on the opposite wall.

Desperately, I tried to remember the Bible verse I'd been claiming. Finally, it came to me—Psalm 112:7. Closing my eyes, I leaned my head against the wall and repeated to myself, "He shall not be afraid of evil tidings: his heart is fixed, trusting in the LORD" (KJV).

For some reason, I had misinterpreted that text. Looking back, its meaning seems too plain to misunderstand, but I certainly had it mixed up then! In my mind, it meant, *Nothing evil will come to the one whose heart is steadfast, trusting in the Lord.*

Our hearts are fixed, aren't they? We are trusting in God, aren't we? Then certainly, God will grant us a good verdict from the doctor!

The door finally opened, and the doctor stepped into the room. I tried to read his impassive face but couldn't. He sat on a stool, stethoscope draped around his neck, and turned to the telephone to get my mom's reports. This was it! The moment we'd been dreading, yet anxiously waiting for.

The doctor hung up the receiver and leaned forward, three pairs of expectant eyes fixed on his face.

"I'm afraid that my news isn't the best." He cleared his throat and paused. *This isn't going according to plan. Come on, Jill, keep your heart fixed on Jesus. You want a good verdict for your mom.* The doctor kept right on talking. "I'm afraid that you *do* have multiple sclerosis. I'm very sorry."

Even though it's been well over a decade since we heard the verdict in that bleak office, I can still recall the details as if it happened yesterday. How my mom's eyes filled with tears. The slump of my dad's shoulders as he bowed his head. The total silence in the room. Over the beating of my heart, I heard that Bible verse. *What has happened to our faith? What has happened to my keeping my heart fixed on Jesus?*

Over the next couple of days, I went back to that psalm and realized that I had most definitely misinterpreted the verse! God wasn't saying that trouble wouldn't come, just that we didn't have to be afraid of it. If I kept my heart and mind focused on Jesus when sickness and disease *did* come, He would keep me from being afraid. He would comfort my heart and grant me His peace.

It's been almost fourteen years since my mom's multiple sclerosis diagnosis, and our precious Savior has granted peace through each turn of the journey.

Fear—it's everywhere. As women, we fear loss of control, loss of loved ones, loss of our own lives; we worry about wearing the right thing, saying the right thing, and doing the right thing; we agonize over our children's choices, our spouse's choices, and our own choices. Fear can spill over into every area of our lives.

FEARS ABOUT HEALTH

God created us to live happy, healthy lives. He told us in 3 John 1:2,

"Beloved, I pray that you may prosper in all things and be in health, just as your soul prospers." How He longs for us to be happy, to be at peace with Him and with our brothers and sisters, to feel good. I believe He has given us natural laws—laws by which His creation is governed—that will greatly improve our health if we follow them.

Having said that, I also know that we live in a world of sin. After Adam and Eve sinned, this world began to experience pain, suffering, and death for the very first time. Can you imagine how Eve felt when she picked a flower and it wilted and died? Or when Adam and Eve saw the first leaf fall off of a tree or when they had to take one of their innocent lambs and cut its throat for the first sacrifice?

Years later, we still shudder a bit as we imagine their pain. We see it as a mom bends low over her suffering child, wishing she could take his pain away. We feel it as we hear the squeal of a tire and feel the impact of metal crunching on metal. We sense it as we walk the halls of a pediatric oncology ward and see precious children, eyes filled with hope even as their bodies waste away.

Fear. *Will that happen to my child? Will it happen to my spouse? Will it happen to me?*

Every week, when Greg and I have our Sabbath-evening sundown vespers, we kneel down by our little couch to pray. The prayer varies greatly from week to week, but one part of the prayer is consistent. Each week, Greg prays something like this: "God, we don't know what we'll face this coming week. We surrender ourselves anew into Your hands. Help us to live each day for You, each moment with our hearts right with You and with each other, for we don't know when our last day will be." That's the beauty of surrender, of living each moment with Jesus, with your face turned toward His, basking in His presence, His love, and in His peace.

For years, if Greg was late coming home from an appointment or work, I would worry that maybe he'd had a car wreck. My mind would plan what I'd say if the hospital called, how I would tell our families, what I would say at his funeral. Fear would clutch at my heart as I tried to imagine life without him. Greg was my everything—my best friend, my prayer partner, and my soul mate! How does one prepare for something like that?

Then, in the midst of my panic, God would gently remind me, *"Jill, think about what is true"* (see Philippians 4:8).

It always made me ask myself, *What really is true?* I didn't know for sure that Greg had been in a wreck; I was simply surmising. So I'd take my thoughts captive to Jesus Christ and claim Isaiah 26:3: "You will keep him in perfect peace, whose mind is stayed on You, because he trusts in You." *OK, Lord, I'm choosing to think on what is true. I'm choosing to think about You.*

Pretty soon I'd see the lights of his pickup shine across the yard, and I'd hurry to finish dinner as he'd walk in the door.

"Oh, sweetie, sorry I was late. So-and-so stopped by to talk just as I was leaving work."

As we read through Psalm 23, it's interesting to see the progression of the psalmist's thoughts. Verse 3 says, "He [the Lord] restores my soul; He leads me in the paths of righteousness for His name's sake." Then, it continues with, "Yea, though I walk through the valley of the shadow of death, I will fear no evil; for You are with me" (verse 4).

As Jesus restores the broken places in my heart and life, as He leads me in His pathway and clothes me with His righteousness, then, and only then, am I able to face the valley of the shadow of death with peace. It's all about relinquishing control, letting go, and letting God take charge of my life. What a beautiful truth that is!

FEARS ABOUT RELATIONSHIPS

One of my favorite Bible books is Psalms. It runs the whole gamut of emotions, yet constantly comes back to God—His presence, His joy, and His incredible love for us, His children.

Psalm 27:1 says,

> The LORD is my light and my salvation;
> Whom shall I fear?
> The LORD is the strength of my life;
> Of whom shall I be afraid?

How often I fear people—what they say, what they think, and what they'll do. But God says, *"I am with you, My daughter. You don't have to be afraid of anyone or anything! I am your strength, your life, your everything."*

Maybe you feel betrayed by a friend, or maybe your spouse is threatening divorce.

Maybe your kids are talking back and acting out, and you're afraid they might leave the church or, worse yet, leave God.

Maybe you're afraid to leave the abusive relationship you're in, or are afraid to tell others about the one you've already left behind.

Maybe you're afraid to step out and speak for God. After all, what would people say or think?

Maybe you're afraid to reach out and make a friend because you've been hurt so many times in the past.

Oh, my sister, God loves you! He has a beautiful plan for your life.

He wants to give you hope and a future (Jeremiah 29:11).

He longs for you to come to Him, just now, just as you are (Matthew 11:28).

He wants to exchange your rags for His garment that is whiter than snow (Isaiah 1:18).

He longs to give you a new heart (Ezekiel 36:26).

He wants to put a new song in your life (Psalm 40:3).

He longs to give you the strength and the grace to walk each day without fear (Psalm 56:3).

FEARS ABOUT THE FUTURE

Fortunately, most of the things we fear never occur. Most of what I worry about has never taken place.

God knew that our hearts and minds would be fearful, so when Jesus walked this earth, He sought to calm our fears. In the Sermon on the Mount, He talked about the lilies and the birds—they didn't worry about their next meal, they didn't wonder if the sun would come up again to warm them, they didn't ponder if they'd lose their beautiful plumage or their fragrant flowers. They simply sat there and bloomed. They simply flew and sang. They simply trusted. Then, turning to the people He loved, Jesus added, "Wherefore, if God so clothe the grass of the field, which to day is, and to morrow is cast into the oven, shall he not much more clothe you, O ye of little faith?" (Matthew 6:30, KJV).

How He loves us! How He desires us to learn to walk with Him, day by day, simply trusting in His plan for our lives, resting in His goodness.

GOD'S SOLUTION

Will we lose our job or our car or our home? Perhaps.

Will someone we love be hurt, injured, or even killed? Maybe.

Is our life guaranteed? No, at least not on this planet we temporarily call home.

Does any of that really matter? No.

Could God save us from any of that if He so chose? Absolutely. After all, He's said, "I am the LORD, the God of all flesh. Is there anything too hard for Me?" (Jeremiah 32:27).

When we come down to it, all that really matters is that we face whatever comes hand in hand with Jesus; that we can still trust Him when everything is crumbling around us; that we don't serve Him for what we get, but that we serve Him for who He is. Because we love Him, because He's good; because where would we go if we didn't have Him?

Oswald Chambers asks, "Have we come to the point where God can withdraw His blessings from us without our trust in Him being affected?"[1]

Do we serve Jesus because He's Santa Claus, giving us what we want, when we want it? Or do we simply serve Him because we love Him, because life without Him would be unthinkable, because nothing in this world really matters except walking through life with Him?

WHAT DO WE KNOW?

So when it comes to fear, what do we know?

God walks with us through everything. Whatever you're going through, He's there. Whatever you're facing, He's there. Whatever trial you have, He's in the midst of it.

One of my favorite promises is found in Isaiah 43:1–3. Our Savior has promised,

> "Fear not [insert your name here], for I have redeemed you;
> I have called you by your name;
> You are Mine.
> When you pass through the waters, I will be with you;
> And through the rivers, they shall not overflow you.
> When you walk through the fire, you shall not be burned,
> Nor shall the flame scorch you.
> For I am the LORD your God,
> The Holy One of Israel, your Savior."

God grants us His peace. Are you tempted? He will deliver. Are you struggling? He will bring comfort. Are you afraid? He will bring peace.

He's promised, "Peace I leave with you, My peace I give to you; not as the world gives do I give to you. Let not your heart be troubled, neither let it be afraid" (John 14:27).

God gives us strength. If you're feeling weak, He'll give strength. If you're frightened, He'll bring courage. If you're helpless, He'll bring deliverance.

> " 'Fear not, for I am with you;
> Be not dismayed, for I am your God.
> I will strengthen you,
> Yes, I will help you,
> I will uphold you with My righteous right hand' " (Isaiah 41:10).

Praise Him. When you don't see a way out, thank Him. When you're lost and alone, praise Him. When you're facing your fear, rejoice in Him.

> Whenever I am afraid,
> I will trust in You.
> In God (I will praise His word),
> In God I have put my trust;
> I will not fear.
> What can flesh do to me? (Psalm 56:3, 4).

Sometimes praise is a hard thing—especially when you don't feel like it or when you're feeling frightened and alone. However, we know that God inhabits the praises of His people (Psalm 22:3). As we thank God for His goodness, as we magnify Him and focus on Him, our problems sink into insignificance. We focus less on self and more on our Savior. Praise changes our perspectives, our thoughts, and, eventually, our feelings.

It won't last forever. "Weeping may endure for a night, but joy comes in the morning" (Psalm 30:5).

Jesus is right by your side. He loves you. He's holding you. He will bring you through!

---

1. Oswald Chambers, "October 23: Nothing of the Old Life!" in *My Utmost for His Highest* (Grand Rapids, Mich.: Discovery House Pub., 1992).

PART 4

Sadness

Chapter 6

A HEART THAT'S *SAD*

Weeping may endure for a night, but joy comes in the morning.
—PSALM 30:5

The phone rang. I pulled my hands out of the bread dough and gingerly picked it up.

"Hello, this is Jill." I cocked my head to the side to hold the phone, and began to rinse my hands at the kitchen sink.

"Yes, Jill, this is Doctor So-and-so." Our doctor! Instantly, I forgot all about my dirty hands. *Why is he calling now? Is this the long-awaited verdict?*

My mind traveled back through the years. From the start, we believed that God had brought us together. Greg and I had earnestly prayed, had searched our hearts, and had sought godly counsel from those who knew us best. What joy, what peace there is in knowing God has handpicked your spouse for you!

We started our journey a bit innocent, a bit naive, yet hand in hand with Jesus. The first major bump hit a couple of years down the road. Most couples decide they want children, and soon their homes are filled with giggles, whimpers, sticky hands, runny noses, hide-and-seek, and childish prattle. However, as weeks became months, our home remained quiet. The negative tests laid flat on the bathroom countertop seemed to mock us. Not pregnant. *Why, God?*

We waited a year. After all, isn't that what all the books suggest? So we read and waited, prayed and waited, then worried and waited. Our hopes rose each month, only to be dashed again.

Soon the round of doctors and tests began—and another round of waiting. We clung to each other and to God. Surely, He would give us the desires of our hearts. After all, weren't the promises in His Word true? Hadn't we proved Him before? We just needed more faith, or did we?

The local doctors sent us to the fertility experts in St. Louis. More doctors. More tests. More waiting. We became afraid to have faith, afraid to claim the promises in His Word; for what if the answer was No? Were we willing to surrender our desires and accept God's will?

The months slipped by. We quit buying that little test from Walmart. Somehow it was easier to not get excited, only to be discouraged again. We constantly reached out to God, and I honestly don't remember feeling angry, just hurt and confused.

Now, unexpectedly, the doctor was on the phone. This was our answer! How do you delay that moment of reckoning? How do you buy time, because, somehow, the unknown is easier to bear than a flat-out No? The doctor kept right on talking, despite my unspoken protests. He was gentle (as gentle as doctors can be) and used words such as *rare, infertile,* and the most confusing ones, "We just don't know why."

He ended with, "I'm very sorry, ma'am." A click, a dial tone, and I was left holding the phone. *Why couldn't he have called when Greg was home?* Greg was at work, and I just couldn't blurt that type of news out over the phone. It would have to wait until dinnertime. How could I get through the afternoon?

Leaving my bread dough, I blindly left the house, tears cascading down my face. I don't remember walking down our driveway, but I do remember turning onto our gravel country road. The leaves were just unfurling their springtime green; overhead, the sky was a perfect blue; the birds flitted from tree to tree, glad to be free from the dearth of winter. All nature seemed in perfect harmony with the Creator, but I couldn't see it, hear it, or sense it. All I felt was the hurt, the pain, and the devastation of my dashed hopes and dreams.

In agony, my spirit cried out to God. He listened quietly until my tears began to ebb and I ran out of words. Then, in the quietness, I heard His voice: *"Jill, My precious daughter, count your blessings."*

What? Had I heard right? I wanted sympathy, and God was concerned with praise? *But God,* I argued, *I don't have anything to be thankful for!*

In the silence, over the beating of my own heart, I heard nothing, then, quietly, *"Jill, My precious daughter, count your blessings."*

Puzzled, but truly wanting to follow God, I searched my mind for my blessings. I spoke them aloud, hesitantly at first, but growing ever stronger. Faster and faster, they tumbled out: my husband, our home, our marriage, our family and friends, our church, our ministry. Oh, I actually did have a lot to be thankful for!

Soon, my praise centered around God: His faithfulness and compassion, His unfailing, unconditional love, His patience and His wisdom, His Word and the promises it contained. Joy began to flicker amid the ashes of my heart. The rainbow began to emerge after the rain. Suddenly, I heard the birds and felt the warmth of the sun on my face. I reached up to touch a tiny green leaf and marveled at the miracle of spring.

And then, I sensed Him. He'd been there all along, only my eyes had been so blinded by tears that I had failed to notice Him. Jesus walked beside me on that gravel road and brought with Him the sunshine of His presence.

SORROWS WE FACE

I don't know what pain or sorrow you've faced in your life. Maybe you're grieving the loss of a loved one, and the pain is so sharp and deep you can hardly breathe. Perhaps you're in the midst of a painful divorce, and death seems easier than life. Or maybe you're walking under gray clouds, and a perpetual mist obscures the sun from view. Whatever the case, know that our Father is "compassionate and merciful" (James 5:11), that underneath are His "everlasting arms" (Deuteronomy 33:27), that He's longing to strengthen you and carry you through.

SORROW FROM LOSS

Theirs was a tight-knit home. Oh, they had differences, as all siblings do. And yes, they'd definitely had spats. But, somehow, they'd grown closer through them.

Surprisingly, as they grew older, they hadn't grown apart. In a large part, this was due to their deepening friendship with a Man like none other. Some called Him Rabbi; others called Him Master; still others called Him Lord.

They'd often entertained this Jesus of Nazareth in their home, along with all twelve of His disciples. Initially, Lazarus had played host, Martha the hostess and servant, and Mary the humble suppliant and student. However, the role Jesus played in their lives, the place He took in their hearts,

HEARTLIFT

had grown through time. No longer was He an ordinary guest or even an honored friend. He'd become their best Friend, their Master and Lord, their Messiah.

One day, Lazarus came home looking flushed. Martha, ever the busy, active sister, took one look at him and got him into bed. It was probably nothing more than a cold, but it never hurt to take extra precautions. The Bible doesn't tell us how long Lazarus lay ill, but there came a day when Mary and Martha both knew the truth: their beloved brother was not sick with a cold; he was very ill and might die without a miracle.

In my imagination, I can see them: eyes red with weeping, hushed voices filled with urgency, hearts full of dread. Mary sitting by Lazarus's bed, wringing out a cloth to place on his fevered forehead; Martha commissioning a servant to carry a swift message to the Master.

The Bible simply records that the two sisters sent a message to Jesus saying, "Lord, behold, he whom You love is sick" (John 11:3). One can only imagine the urgency of that appeal. However, instead of leaving immediately for Bethany, Jesus lingered.

Why?

Didn't He love Lazarus and Martha and Mary? Absolutely (verse 5).

Did he want Lazarus to die, and Mary and Martha to endure such grief? No, He never delights in suffering.

Jesus Himself gave the explanation: "This sickness is not unto death, but for the glory of God, that the Son of God may be glorified through it" (verse 4). Did Jesus know Lazarus would die? Of course He did. He was simply stating that God was working all things out for good, so that His glory might be revealed. If He had healed the sick Lazarus, that would have been a small miracle and, most certainly, a blessing. But when He raised the dead Lazarus back to life, the news of that miracle was unstoppable.

However, the sisters didn't know any of that. All they knew was that Jesus hadn't come. Anxiously, they watched the road for signs of Him as their beloved brother slipped away. Why, oh why hadn't Jesus answered their plea? Didn't He love them?

Sorrowfully, they prepared Lazarus for burial. Painfully, they watched the stone being rolled in front of the tomb. Dolefully, they listened to the cries of the mourners and longed for Jesus.

Finally, four days after the burial, Jesus showed up. We know how that story ended; but to me, the most precious part of the story comes in verse

58

35. When Jesus saw the Jews weeping, when He saw Martha and Mary weeping, He asked where Lazarus was buried. Then is revealed our Savior's compassion: "Jesus wept" (verse 35).

What an incredible Savior we have! He knew He was going to raise Lazarus from the dead in just a moment; He knew this wasn't the end but only the beginning; He knew their weeping would be turned into rejoicing—yet He sorrowed still.

I believe He wept because of the depth of their pain, because of their crushing sorrow, because they were His friends, and He hated to see them suffer.

Are you watching someone you love suffer right now? Is cancer or some other disease diminishing his or her body, gradually snuffing out life? Are your days filled with crushing sorrow, your nights long and unbearable? Know that the Lord Jesus is sitting right beside you, mingling His tears with yours. He hurts because you hurt, because your pain is deep, because your loss is unfathomable. He's asking you to come to Him just now, weak and burdened, and He will give you His rest (Matthew 11:28). He longs to lift the weight from your shoulders, to give you grace to endure, and to grant you peace in the process. Not only that, He wants to turn your sorrow into joy (John 16:20).

Perhaps your loss doesn't stem from someone's death. Perhaps you're dealing with the loss of a dream: that job you always wanted, the marriage you never had, the health you always hoped for, the money you never had, the house you wanted to live in, or the children you could never have.

In the midst of our infertility journey, Greg wrote a question and shared it with me. It simply said, "How do you let go of something you never had?" That's true, not just for us, but for anyone anywhere who is dealing with loss. How do you surrender what was never yours in the first place?

Perhaps you're dealing with the devastation of your children's choices. *At what point did I begin to lose them?* you wonder. *When did they start to turn away from Jesus?*

One of my friends has dealt with this pain for years. It began when her son informed her he was gay and was choosing to live a gay lifestyle. Oh, the sleepless nights; the devastation of a mom's hopes and dreams; the pain of the question, Will he return to the Lord before it's too late? Even as I write this, he's still living that lifestyle, but his mom hasn't given up hope. She's still storming the gates of heaven on his behalf, pleading the Word of God over his life, hoping that someday, somehow, he'll choose to come home.

Before we discuss God's solution for our sorrow and pain, let's look at some other types of sorrow.

SORROW FROM CHOICE

An anguished cry burst forth in the Sanhedrin's chambers. Instantly, the low buzz of conversation ceased. Dozens of priestly eyes looked up. *Why, this is the disciple who just sold Jesus to us. What's his name? Ah, that's right. Judas.*

I can imagine Caiaphas looking scornfully at the troubled man. "What do you want with us? You got your money, didn't you?" He waves his hand. "Be gone with you."

Suddenly, the tinkling sound of coins fills the room as Judas flings the thirty pieces of silver at the high priest's feet. "I never should have sold Jesus. He's innocent! Innocent, I tell you!"

The priests' eyes flash with anger. *How dare that disciple reveal our bribery?* " 'What do we care?' they retorted. 'That's your problem' " (Matthew 27:4, NLT).

In great agony, Judas left their chambers and went out and hanged himself (verse 5). His sorrow didn't stem from a great love for Jesus or from a conviction that he had just sold the Son of God. He was only sorry that Jesus hadn't freed Himself and set up His earthly kingdom, disappointed that his plans had gone awry, upset that his conniving and greed had failed to achieve his heart's desire. The choices Judas made, while seemingly small and insignificant, had led him on, step by step, to this supreme sorrow of heart and soul.

Sorrow from choice looks a bit hard, doesn't it? Cold. *If you have sorrow or problems, you must have brought it on yourself.* Well, not always. I believe there are two ways we can experience this pain.

First, we experience sorrow from the poor choices we make. Judas is an example of this type of sorrow. When my friend Mollie teaches our class on Sabbath, she frequently refers to the law of sowing and reaping (Galatians 6:7, 8). We reap what we sow. If we sow selfishness, revenge, and jealousy, then we reap a bountiful harvest of broken relationships, bitterness of soul, and betrayal. If we sow love, kindness, and forgiveness, we reap a beautiful harvest of friendship, peace, and joy. One type of sowing leads to sorrow; the other to joy.

This type of sowing doesn't apply just to emotions and feelings. We can also sow poor decisions, such as choosing an ungodly spouse ("Oh, I'll change him once we're married."), poor business choices ("Get-rich-quick schemes don't work for most people, but I'll be the exception."), choices in entertainment ("I'm strong in Jesus, so I can watch anything or go anywhere and not be affected."). Yes, God can work good out of any situation—even those we get into ourselves—but the consequences of our choices are always there (Romans 8:28).

Second, we experience sorrow by not responding to trials and afflictions in God's way. Let me explain. Yes, we all have sorrow; we all experience loss. Granted, some trials are much harder to bear than others. Yet, whom do we turn to in our grief? Do we wallow in it, even as it turns into self-pity and bitterness of spirit, or do we choose to surrender, to allow God to come in and do His work in our hearts?

I believe that sorrow from loss can turn us in two different directions: either it leads us closer to God—and eventually to fullness of joy and "pleasures forevermore"—or it leads us away from God and into Satan's trap of self-pity, bitterness, and depression (Psalm 16:11).

Have you ever met someone who was a "victim" of sorrow from choice—someone with a multitude of problems, a litany of excuses, a woe-is-me mentality? I've talked with women who have been divorced for years, whose pain, bitterness, and resentment is just as fresh, or even stronger, as the day their divorces were final. They've indulged their vindictive spirits, their self-righteousness ("After all, he's the one who had the affair!"), their sense of being wronged, until their minds become hamster wheels, turning on one topic only. Continually angry. Constantly depressed.

Then I've met other women who have been deeply hurt, yet still seem to radiate joy. They seek new ways to minister for Jesus. They reach out to others who have been hurt, desiring to bring them comfort, just as they were "comforted by God" (2 Corinthians 1:3, 4). These women chose Jesus' way of turning sorrow into joy and peace.

GOD'S SOLUTION

From the beginning, when our first parents were forced from their Eden home, pain has been a part of life. Eve saw the first leaf fall, the first lamb slaughtered, the first murder committed (and that, by her own son). She, who had been a stranger to pain, became intimately acquainted with it. And since that day, suffering and sorrow have spread in the wake of sin. I know each one of you has experienced your own anguish of heart. None of us are exempt.

However, the future is not bleak. Not only do we have the hope of eternal life with our Savior, in which He will "wipe away every tear" from our eyes, but we can experience His fullness of joy here and now (Revelation 21:4). He so longs to grant us a garment of praise in exchange for our spirit of heaviness (Isaiah 61:3). I know. I've seen the transformation He's made in my own heart and in the hearts of my friends. You can have joy and peace in Jesus!

Here are the principles that God used to effect the change in my own heart. I know your path is different from mine. That's OK. Just know that God is willing to work in your heart, transforming your sorrow to joy. He can be depended on to complete the work He's begun (Philippians 1:6).

Allow yourself time to grieve. We often try to rush the healing process—both our own, and someone else's. We ask, "Why am I not feeling better?" just two weeks after a tragic loss.

It takes time to heal, time to allow God to pour the oil of His Holy Spirit into your wounded heart. Let Him do the heart work that's needed. Don't rush yourself. Don't stuff your emotions. Allow Him to work through them, one by one.

Surrender your sadness, your thoughts, to God. This step is painful, but oh so important. Remember Christ in the Garden of Gethsemane? He earnestly pleaded, sweating drops of blood, that the bitter cup should pass from Him. How His humanity shrank from that final great sacrifice, from that separation from His Father. But from His pale, quivering lips came that cry, "O My Father, if this cup cannot pass away from Me unless I drink it, Your will be done" (Matthew 26:42). Even the Son of God chose to surrender. Only when we surrender can God work in us to transform us.

Remember the infertility journey Greg and I faced? It seems like nothing in comparison with Jesus' sacrifice, yet it still required surrender. *Yes, Father, we trust You. If we can serve You better, if Your overreaching plan is for us to not have children, we choose to accept that.* Choose to surrender.

What release there is in surrender! I'm not saying God causes the evil that happens in our world. Far from it. But our God is so big that He can take any situation Satan throws our way and works it out for good (Romans 8:28). Because He loves us. Because He's good.

What if you're single, but would love to be married? Surrender that desire to Jesus. Choose to serve Him and follow Him while you're still single.

What if your child has left the Lord? Surrender him or her to Jesus. You can't control the outcome. You can't keep your child in church. You can only release him or her to Jesus, and ask Him to do what you can't do yourself.

Practice thankfulness. I believe this step is where the battle is fought—and the victory is won!

A thankful heart has a "continual feast" (Proverbs 15:15)! Do you want to feast? Then practice giving thanks, thinking thanks, speaking thanks.

They say practice makes perfect, but I believe practice makes permanent. If you practice negative thinking, if you nurse sadness, self-pity, or bitterness, your mind will become accustomed to thinking and speaking that way. However, the opposite also holds true. Choose to take every thought captive to the Lord Jesus (2 Corinthians 10:5). Practice 1 Thessalonians 5:16–18: "Rejoice always, pray without ceasing, in everything give thanks; for this is the will of God in Christ Jesus for you." Notice Paul doesn't say everything is thankworthy. Of course, it isn't. But we can choose a thankful heart, a thankful spirit. We can practice thankfulness until it becomes a habit.

This is where I fought the battle with my feelings of loss over our infertility. I'd go to buy a baby gift for a friend's shower, and Satan would creep in with self-pity. Just as surely, the Holy Spirit would remind me, *"Jill, My daughter, give thanks."* So, standing there in the aisle beside bottles, rubber duckies, and onesies, I'd thank God for my friend's joy. I'd enumerate *my* blessings: money to buy a gift, the ability to drive to the store, my eyesight, the gift of my friend, the joy of Jesus, the blessing of a wonderful husband, a wonderful ministry God has called me to.

Praise God, self-pity cannot endure a praise party! Pretty soon, the joy of the Lord would flood my soul and give me strength (Nehemiah 8:10). God was waiting to give me the victory, but I needed to make that choice of giving thanks (1 Corinthians 15:57).

I love Habakkuk 3:17–19. However, it begins with some pretty depressing stuff:

> Though the fig tree may not blossom,
> Nor fruit be on the vines;
> Though the labor of the olive may fail,

And the fields yield no food;
Though the flock may be cut off from the fold,
And there be no herd in the stalls (verse 17).

Sounds pretty bad, doesn't it? They faced horrible economic hardships and had every right to be sad. Or did they? Habakkuk continues,

Yet I will rejoice in the LORD,
I will joy in the God of my salvation.
The LORD God is my strength;
He will make my feet like deer's feet,
and He will make me walk on my high hills (verses 18, 19).

Are you facing financial collapse or even bankruptcy? Choose to thank God anyway. Are you enduring loss and wallowing in self-pity? Begin now to praise Jesus anyway. Is your health poor? Count your blessings. No matter what's going on, choose to rejoice in Jesus. And as you rejoice, God will transform your heart.

Spend time in God's Word. The Bible contains so many promises—so much that you and I can meditate on, pray over, and claim for our daily walk with Jesus! My friend J. D. recommends taking three-by-five-inch index cards and writing out a promise on each one. Pick specific promises—ones that will encourage you to choose Jesus and keep pressing on. Try Psalm 40:2, 3. Write it out on your card. Put your name in the verse. Pull your card out often and reread, meditate, and memorize it. This psalm says, "He [God] also brought me up out of a horrible pit, out of the miry clay, and set my feet upon a rock" (verse 2). Are you in a pit? Do you feel like your feet are in quicksand, that there is no way out? Jesus will pull you out; He will set your feet up on a rock. But He's not finished there. The next verse says,

He has put a new song in my mouth—
Praise to our God;
Many will see it and fear,
And will trust in the LORD (verse 3).

God is the One who can put praise in your heart, praise on your lips. And why does He do it? So people can say how wonderful you are? No.

A HEART THAT'S *SAD*

He does it so others can observe the transformation of your life—from sorrow to joy—and learn to trust in God, as well, so God's power, glory, and character can be revealed. Praise His name! If He can transform us, surely He can transform someone else, as well!

Develop friendships with women. Sadness thrives in solitude. Reach out to other women. Join a support group. Start a Bible study on grief in your own home. Be accountable. Be willing to step out of your comfort zone and ask for help when you need it.

As women, God places us in friendships and community for a purpose. It's not so we can simply sit and chatter about the latest clothes, music, and restaurants. Nor is it so we can sit and gossip. He places us together so we can encourage, pray with, and support each other; so we can share with each other what Jesus has done in our own lives; so we can minister together. Reach out to another hurting sister, and begin that cycle of transformation all over again.

Serve God—don't just keep busy. There's a vast difference between the two, you know. Sometimes, we run from our sadness, stuffing our emotions by a constant round of activity, always working—and apparently successful.

The problem is that busyness can be just a facade. It's a way to keep out those who are closest to us, a way to stuff our emotions, a way to avoid surrender, the giving of thanks, and real relationships with other women.

Go to God. Ask Him where your heart is right now. Are you simply keeping busy to avoid your pain? Or are you choosing to surrender, to give thanks, to walk in community *while* serving God? If it's the latter, then praise Him! Bloom right where He's planted you. Serve Him with all your heart, soul, and mind (Matthew 22:37). Blessings will be poured into your life as you do!

Focus on others. Ask God to open your eyes to the needs of those around you. Seek for ways to serve. Observe when a friend is hurting. Pray with her and for her. Lift up those who are weary, pray for those who are oppressed, encourage those who are struggling. Make a phone call, send a card, stop by and visit a fellow church member in need. If you have money, share with those less fortunate; if you have time, give of yourself; if you have neither, then seek for other ways to serve—even in small ways.

As you think of others and work for their salvation, God will heap joy and abundant blessings on you. Truly, "it is more blessed to give than to receive" (Acts 20:35).

3—H.L.

Finally, God will bring joy. We began this chapter with the promise in Psalm 30:5: "Weeping may endure for a night, but joy comes in the morning."

I used to think that promise only applied to eternity: *yes, there is sorrow on this earth, but we'll have to wait for joy until Jesus returns.*

While I still believe we'll be joyful in heaven, I believe this promise also applies to us on this earth, in the here and now. As we choose God's way of dealing with loss, He will bring peace and joy back into our hearts. His joy is not dependent on circumstances. Jesus' type of joy is constant, no matter what we are experiencing.

As Greg and I surrendered our hearts to God, as we learned to practice giving thanks, as we focused on the needs of others, our faithful God poured the oil of His Holy Spirit into our hurting hearts and brought about healing and grace. We began to learn, and are still learning, some beautiful lessons in faith, trust, and total surrender and submission to our Father's will. What began as a "Why us, God?" slowly turned into a "Why not us, God?"

Do we praise our heavenly Father only when He answers our prayers as we desire? Shouldn't we be just as content, just as faithful, and just as trusting whether the answer is what we originally wanted or not?

I'm not sure when the change occurred, but God did it! He's led us to a place of total contentment in His will, given us joy in this journey, and opened doors for ministry while fulfilling the desires of our hearts with much more than we could ever have imagined. How happy we are that God has revealed His will for our lives. What a joy to know we're in the place He wants us to be, doing exactly what He's called us to do—and loving it!

Dear reader, our Father is reaching out to you just now in love. He's saying, "Come to Me, My daughter. I'll take your pain and grief and replace it with My peace, with My joy."

Surrender is never easy, and giving thanks can be painful at first. But persevere! Don't give up! As you press closer into His presence, you will experience His fullness of joy (Psalm 16:11).

PART 5

Purity

A HEART THAT
FANTASIZES

*Put on the Lord Jesus Christ, and make no provision for the flesh,
to fulfill its lusts.*

—ROMANS 13:14

The air felt stifling hot. Oppressive. She sighed as she glanced out the window. The sun stood almost overhead. It was time.[1]

Grabbing her water pot, she quietly slipped out the door. Maybe if she kept out of sight, away from the marketplace, from the open stares, the whispered jabs, it would be easier. She pulled her robe tighter about her and hurried down the path.

Too late! She'd been discovered. Mothers grabbed their children and pressed their little faces tightly against their own garments, seeking to shield their pure eyes from her filth. Head high, eyes blinded by tears, she stumbled past, trying to ignore their taunts and jeers. *They used to be my neighbors—my friends.* But that was so long ago. Before she went through more husbands than a kid could count. Before she became a dirty, defiled, disgraced woman. Before—oh, she didn't like to think about it.

When was the last time she felt pure? She couldn't remember. It seemed as if her life had always been filled with men taking advantage of her, using her, then throwing her out like a piece of worthless trash. But then, she didn't deserve anything better. No upright man ever wanted her.

All she had ever longed for was a man to love her, a man to hold her and tell her she was beautiful. So she had allowed them into her life, trying desperately to hold on to someone—anyone—who would fill that void in her aching heart. But none of them ever had: not one of her five husbands, not the boyfriends in between, nor her current live-in boyfriend. Each encounter left her feeling more used, dirtier than ever.

She stumbled on the path. Glancing up, she realized she was almost at the well. *Wait a minute; there's a man sitting at the well!* This was why she always came at noon, so she could be alone—alone with her thoughts, alone with her hurt, alone with her fears. *What is he doing here? And his robe? Definitely Jewish!*

She swiped at her tears with the back of her hand. Eyes downcast, she approached the well. *The sooner I get out of here, the better.*

As she lowered the bucket, He spoke. "Excuse Me, ma'am, would you be so kind as to give Me a drink of water?"

Nervously, she tugged on the rope. *What a kind voice he has.* She couldn't remember the last time she'd been treated so respectfully. *He's probably trying to use me, like all the other men I've met.* She shrugged her shoulders without looking up. "You're a Jew, why are you asking me for a drink of water? I'm just a Samaritan, and a woman at that."

As He answered, she dared to lift her head. Why, He was looking right at her. Such kind eyes. Such purity! Such power! And, amazingly, there was none of the usual contempt, the usual condemnation that greeted her wherever she went. All she saw was compassion and love. Not lust—oh, she was used to that. This was different. Somehow this Man looked at her as if she were innocent and pure. He didn't seem to see all that filth clinging to her.

The cup trembled in her hand as she held it out to Him. He was speaking of living water. Oh, if she could only drink some too! And then the hope she had allowed herself to feel was crushed. "Go," He said, "call your husband, and bring him here."

Did she have to tell this kind Man about her sinful lifestyle, about her degradation? Oh, He would look at her like all the other people did. He'd shun her.

She lowered her voice. "I have no husband," she whispered, unable to meet His eyes.

"I know," He said, with infinite compassion. "You've had five husbands, and you're not married to the man you're living with now."

How does He know? Who told Him? He is a total stranger! As she glanced up, she saw Him looking at her with the same expression of love and compassion. Knowledge of her sin made no difference. He still loved her. He still saw her as she could be—purified and forgiven. What a miracle of grace!

MY PERSONAL BATTLE

To be honest with you, this has not been an easy chapter for me to write. In my own life, I've struggled with impurity more than I care to admit. Oh, I'm not talking about outward things such as kissing men, sleeping around, or even visiting bars or clubs. What I'm talking about is the inward condition of my heart and soul—purity of thought, purity of heart, purity of life. That's where my struggle has been. And whether you've compromised in all of those outward areas, or whether you defiled only your heart and mind—or even if you feel that you've always been virtuous—please don't skip this chapter.

Don't feel despair if you've already fallen. Don't feel discouraged if there's impurity lurking in your heart that you're trying to keep hidden. And don't turn the page if you consider yourself exempt from this struggle and assume you don't need this information.

Our God is longing to cleanse us and set us free—free from the addiction of lust, free from the stain of sin, free from the judgmental spirit toward those who have fallen! I believe God's call to purity of heart and soul and mind is higher, much higher, than you or I could ever imagine. As I draw closer into His presence, I feel as if I'm just beginning to comprehend the purity He intends for His followers.

From childhood, I always had a vivid imagination. My sister and I would play dolls for hours, and I would provide the fodder for the dolls' daily lives. With little outside influences from TV or movies, we developed plays and stories, radio talk shows, sermons, and programs. We didn't need video games (they hadn't been invented back then, anyway)—we just had our imaginations!

As I grew into my teens and young adulthood, Satan took that imagination, which was a gift from God, and began to feed me stories and movies that took my healthy imagination and transformed it into a fantasy, romance world. Anytime I had a pang of conscience, he would spin another of his masterful lies: "Everyone else is watching this movie, and they're all good Christian girls." Or, "This is not a romance novel; it's a Christian novel with just a little romantic story interwoven. Isn't God the Author of love?"

I would decide not to read fiction anymore, and would keep that promise for months and sometimes years. But the stories lived on in my mind. Try as I might, they were very hard to ignore, hard to forget.

Years passed, and I earnestly sought to follow Jesus. God led Greg and me together into courtship, engagement, and marriage. We saved our first kiss for the altar. It was a beautiful love story, and Greg was so incredibly good to me.

We didn't have much money, but we had each other and our commitment to God. Early in our marriage, we decided to buy a little thirteen-inch TV with a rabbit-ears antenna to watch the local news and weather. I was concerned about the purchase because of my attraction to romantic stories and movies; but I rationalized that everyone else in our church watched TV, and they were good Christians. In fact, they preached, taught, and lived the Christian walk better than I did.

Greg enjoyed the news and weather, but I soon latched on to something else—soap operas! They were a good romance novel come to life. High drama, broken hearts, marital infidelity, love, sex, and romance—they had it all. The stories danced right from the screen into my mind, to be replayed and reworked in countless different ways and angles. I was hooked.

I hid my addiction from Greg as best I could. He knew I struggled a bit but had no idea of the intensity of my battle. At least, I didn't think he did, until one evening he asked if we could talk. We talked often, so his request was nothing new. Only he usually didn't broach a subject in that manner.

Sitting down, we faced each other, and he began to share how God had called him to be the priest of our home, how he was responsible to God for the salvation of our family. I sat there, uncertain where this conversation was heading.

Then, he hit on my cherished sin—soap operas. I was stunned! I knew that what I was watching was wrong. I knew they were leading me away from Jesus. I knew there was nothing of Philippians 4:8 present in a single episode. But I was addicted! Try as I could, I couldn't tear myself away.

Greg knew all of this, and God gave him the wisdom, courage, and love to make the right decision for our home. Through the years, I've never forgotten what he said that evening.

"Jilly, God is asking me as priest of our home to get rid of the TV." He knew I didn't have the strength to make that choice on my own, so he led in that decision.

A HEART THAT *FANTASIZES*

We knelt down in front of our little couch and prayed, seeking forgiveness as a couple, asking for strength to throw out our TV, pleading for purity of heart and life.

They say each decision in life, whether great or small, influences other decisions. The decision we made together that night, almost nine years ago, was one of the best decisions of our lives. It started me on that path to purity and peace, holiness and oneness with my Savior. I've never regretted it. And I've always blessed my husband for having the strength to make the difficult decision I couldn't seem to make for myself.

Now, just because we got rid of the TV didn't mean my fantasy world ceased. Controlling my thoughts proved to be an ongoing battle, for those images, those plots, those feelings would pop up at the most inopportune times. But daily, hourly—every other moment, at times—Jesus transformed my life by the renewing of my mind as I surrendered my heart to Him (Romans 12:1, 2).

I believe Satan lays special traps for us in this area of purity. He knows that a woman's heart is tender, vulnerable, and open to deception, so he weaves his web skillfully. While men are visually stimulated—and therefore especially vulnerable to pornography or visual images—women are emotionally stimulated. I believe what porn is to many men, romantic novels, TV programs, and movies are to many women. They may look different, but the end result is the same: a heart pulled away from beholding Jesus, a mind filled with romantic daydreams that aren't true, a soul polluted with lust, a longing for what isn't ours.

GOD'S SOLUTION

I don't know where you are in your journey to purity of heart and life. Whether you're just beginning this journey or are miles down the road, take heart! Jesus loves you and longs to set you free.

I know what it's like to say, "Lord, take my heart. I'm choosing You!" and the next instant be bombarded with an inappropriate or impure thought from my past. For some people, I believe Jesus gives instant release, immediate deliverance. But it didn't work that way for me. It was an intense battle, an earnest hand-to-hand combat; but Jesus gained the victory. Here is how it worked for me—and how it can work for you too:

Step 1. I sought forgiveness. Go to your heavenly Father. After all, He already knows your struggles, your heart's issues, and your lustful thoughts.

Ask Him for forgiveness, for the cleansing blood of Jesus. Claim 1 John 1:9: "If we confess our sins, He is faithful and just to forgive us our sins and to cleanse us from all unrighteousness."

Now get up off your knees, believing you're the purified bride of the King, cleansed, sanctified, and ready for service! Don't waste time doing penance. Simply come as you are, ask for forgiveness, and then go forth in His strength!

Step 2. I surrendered my heart, my thought life, and my emotions. This isn't a once-in-a-lifetime surrender. Steps 2, 3, and 4 are where my battle took place. I would surrender my romantic fantasy to God, only to have it pop back up almost immediately. When a fantasy comes back to you, don't dwell on it! Don't allow yourself to think those thoughts again. Cry out to God for help! He promises, "Before they call, I will answer; and while they are still speaking, I will hear" (Isaiah 65:24).

Also claim 2 Corinthians 10:5 over your life: "Casting down arguments and every high thing that exalts itself against the knowledge of God, bringing every thought into captivity to the obedience of Christ." That verse used to terrify me! Did God mean *every* thought? *Every single thought?* Yes, but He doesn't ask us to do that in our own strength. His grace will be sufficient in your time of weakness (2 Corinthians 12:9). Cling to Him. Surrender, resurrender, and then surrender again! Each time it gets easier. Each time it takes longer before those lustful thoughts resurface.

Step 3. I beheld Jesus. Of all the steps, I believe this is one of the most important. After all, how can we sweep our house and keep it clean without replacing what we pushed out with something—or Someone—else (Matthew 12:43–45)? Look to Jesus! See Him in His purity. Study Jesus' life. Spend time in His Word and with others who are seeking Him. Behold Him as you work, as you drive, as you talk, and your life will be transformed into His image.

I love Romans 12. It begins with Paul's plea for the believers to present their bodies as living sacrifices to God, holy and acceptable. Then verse 2 says, "Do not be conformed to this world, but be transformed [*metamorphosed* in Greek] by the renewing of your mind."

Have you ever seen a caterpillar? Not very attractive, is it? But then a caterpillar forms its cocoon, and pretty soon a metamorphosis takes place, and that caterpillar changes into a beautiful butterfly!

God looks at you and says, "I have a beautiful plan for your life. You're going to be a princess! You might be wallowing in the mud right now, but I want to transform you into a dazzling woman, radiant with My glory and My purity." That's what Jesus can do! Just behold Him.

Step 4. I guarded the avenues of my mind. This is key! We can't strive for purity of heart and life while we constantly feed our romantic fantasies. What we feed grows, and what we starve dies. Starve the untransformed woman and her lusts and passions (Galatians 5:24). Don't watch anything on TV—whether it's a documentary or a movie—that will kindle those old passions and lusts. Don't pick up a book or magazine that will cause those fantasies to spring back to life. Don't listen to anything on the radio, or even a CD, that will fan the flame of lust.

Paul tells us to "put on the Lord Jesus Christ, and make no provision for the flesh, to fulfill its lusts" (Romans 13:14). Just how do we make "no provision for the flesh" in practical terms? By removing the temptation, as far as possible, from our homes. Are you struggling with watching programs on TV that are feeding your romantic fantasies? Get rid of your TV! Is a book from your bookshelf tempting you? Throw it away! Does one of your magazines pull at the lust in your heart? Cancel your subscription!

I know this seems harsh, *but it works.* I used to say I was strong enough in Jesus to keep those books in my home, but I wasn't. I wouldn't read them for a long time; but then, in a weak moment, I'd look in their direction, and there they were, staring me in the face. How much easier to remove that temptation from your home!

Sometimes, it's hard to decide what is acceptable to listen to, to watch, and to read. So submit everything to the test of God's Word. Compare it with Philippians 4:8. Ask yourself, *Is this movie true? Is it honest? Is it pure? Is it virtuous?* As you go down the list, you'll find that many will automatically be eliminated.

Be open to the Holy Spirit's work in your heart and life. Sometimes I'll pick up a biography; but as I begin to read, I feel that old romantic pull in my heart, and I sense that it will pull me away from Jesus. The more you seek His face and desire to follow Him, the more sensitive you will become to His voice. Don't fight the work of the Holy Spirit. Open your heart to Him, and your mind will be transformed!

Step 5. I became accountable. If you're married and your husband is open to God and to talking with you about it, then share with him. Share your frustrations, your struggles, and your need for prayer. If you're single, or uncomfortable sharing with your husband, then find a trusted female friend to pray with, share with, and be accountable to. God puts us in community as believers for a reason. I believe it's so we can lift each other up in prayer, so we can seek God's face together, so we can encourage each other. There's power in united prayer!

Step 6. I stopped comparing myself to others. Recently, I complained to my prayer partner about what I saw as an unfair situation. I'd overheard one of the fifth-graders at school talking about a movie he'd recently seen, and what rankled me was that a ten-year-old was watching something I knew would draw *me* back into that romantic fantasyland. Why did I have to be so strict? Why couldn't I watch it too?

My sister listened and then gently reminded me that I don't need to compare myself with others around me. I'm to look only to Jesus. If someone else can watch a certain movie and be OK with it, then so be it. God asks me only to work out *my own* salvation (Philippians 2:12, 13). God knows the way my heart works, He knows my past struggles with impurity, so He has a special guard over my heart—and that's OK. That's not only OK, it's a blessing!

I don't know where your heart is right now. Lust is a serious topic. I know it's also a difficult one. Keep an open mind and heart to the work the Holy Spirit wants to do in your life. Know that no matter where you've been or how far you've fallen, Jesus longs to stand you up as His purified, cleansed daughter.

You're a princess! Guard your heart. Let our Father hold it in His hands and keep it pure for you. Let Him do the heart work needed so you can stand before the world as a spectacle unto angels and to men of His power, His grace, and His glory (1 Corinthians 4:9)!

---

1. See John 4:5–42.

Chapter 8

A HEART THAT'S
GUARDED

Keep your heart with all diligence, for out of it spring the issues of life.
—PROVERBS 4:23

The sun was just coming up when he stepped out the door. There was a good deal of work to do that day in the fields, and he needed to check on the overseers. Then he would stop at the grain bins and check on the new shipment of cattle after that, and finally head to the house for dinner and the dinner guests. *Does the butler have everything ready?*

He thought back through the years to when he had come to this heathen land as a teenager. So much had changed, but not his love for his God. If anything, it had grown deeper with the trials and hardships, strengthened through much prayer and dependence on his heavenly Father. After all, his earthly father was far, far away. *Is he still alive? Does he still think about me?*

Joseph turned and entered his master Potiphar's home. As he turned down a hallway, he heard a woman's voice.

"Joseph, come here, I want to talk to you," she called out.

Warily, he stood in the doorway to her room. The Bible records that Potiphar's wife simply said, "Lie with me" (Genesis 39:7). What else she might have said, one can only imagine. However, the important part of the story comes with Joseph's response. First, he refuses, then seeks to give her an explanation for his refusal. He refers to the implicit trust Potiphar has in him, and adds that Potiphar has given him everything except his wife. Then he brings out the real reason: "How then can I do this great wickedness, and sin against God?" (verse 9).

Uppermost in Joseph's mind and heart was his relationship to his God. What would please Him? How best could he represent Him? Why should he obey God? Simply because he loved Him. However, Potiphar's wife didn't give up easily. She pressured Joseph daily, and if we study what the Egyptian women wore at that time, we can only imagine the constant battle Joseph was in, not only to say No to her, but to keep his thoughts and mind pure before God. Daily, he chose the high road, the hard road, and said No: No to sin, No to sexual temptation, No to the constant pressures of his workplace.

Then one day she caught him alone in the house. No other men were present. It was just Joseph and her. Grabbing his coat, she begged him again! And fearful that he might give in if he lingered, fearful of his own weakness, he turned and fled.

Now, when you hear the story of Joseph, what do you think of? I think of a man who loved God more than his own desires; a man who chose purity over passion; a man who honored God, even if it might cost him his life itself. What purity! What integrity! What devotion to God! I believe Joseph's story is valuable because it could be *each of us* in this story. Whether men or women, we can choose the path of purity and peace, of surrender and self-denial, of devotion and dedication to God. What a precious testament to the power of God, the power to keep us from sin!

However, let's look at this story from another perspective, from a different angle, through the eyes of Mrs. Potiphar. What was her life like?

Did her husband travel much? Perhaps.

Was she ever lonely? Maybe.

Was she used to getting what she wanted? Most definitely.

We don't know much about her life, yet we do know this: it was probably a life of ease—given her servants and social position in Egypt. She most likely wielded a good deal of influence and control, given her husband's prestigious job and affluence. She obviously was dissatisfied with her life, or at least unhappy with her husband.

Did she try to seduce Joseph because she was bored with life or with her husband? Was it a power struggle to get to Joseph? Was she empty inside, seeking to fill that void with some sense of purpose that Joseph seemed to possess? Or did she simply feed her lust until she desired someone who wasn't hers, someone new and exciting? Whatever the reason, I believe we can learn much from her story.

FIRST, BEWARE OF THE UNGUARDED HEART

The devil is constantly seeking to make us idle. How many times have we heard his whisper? "You've worked hard. Why don't you take a break? Indulge in a little selfish pleasure. You don't have to be so strict all the time. Don't worry about your thoughts for a little while. You can let them drift. You've been so good; you deserve this break."

Run from such thoughts! Turn to Jesus and seek His grace. Don't indulge in idleness, in daydreaming, or anything that will allow your guard to come down.

I was recently talking with one of the women in my congregation who had a special prayer request for diligence—diligence to serve God where He's called her, diligence to get up from the chair and accomplish the work around the house, diligence to pray and study instead of indulge in mind-numbing idleness.

How easy it is to come home from a long day at work and think, *I'll take ten minutes and watch the news. It'll be a time where I can relax and zone out.* Beware! The idle, zoned-out heart is easy prey to Satan's snares. I know. I've been there!

Remember the story of David and Bathsheba? If David had been busy doing his job—doing what God had called him to do as a king—he would have never fallen into Satan's trap. The Bible tells us that "at the time when kings go out to battle, that David sent" his men, yet he remained behind in Jerusalem (2 Samuel 11:1).

Why didn't he go into battle with his soldiers? Perhaps he was tired of fighting. Perhaps he felt that he had done his share. After all, he was king! Let his men do that dirty work of fighting. Whatever the reason, he stayed behind, and Satan took advantage of his idleness, of his vulnerability, and lured him into sin.

Now I'm not saying God doesn't want us to take appropriate rest (Mark 6:31). He desires us to learn of Him because His yoke is easy and His burden is light (Matthew 11:28–30). However, what we do during that resting time makes all the difference.

I might come home from a tiring day, prop my feet up on the couch, open His Word, and spend a few minutes meditating on Him instead of zoning out. I might watch the sunset from my porch while I commune with my Maker, thanking Him for my day. Or I might ask for advice on the problems I encountered and the people I interacted with or simply bask in His presence. Relax, but with Him. It makes all the difference in our lives.

SECOND, BEWARE OF THE DISCONTENTED HEART

Paul tells us that "godliness with contentment is great gain" (1 Timothy 6:6). As we seek God's heart, as we strive to be busy doing what He's called us to do, we can learn to practice contentment with the spouse God has given us. Thank God for your husband. Tell him how much you appreciate him. Look for specific ways to encourage him, to honor him, to build him up. Don't look over the fence at your neighbor's grass. Be thankful for the grass you do have and seek to water it, fertilize it, and help it grow.

I believe that as women we must be so careful in this area. A friend shared with me once how she constantly compared her husband to a friend at work. Perhaps you wish he would work harder and provide better for you, like your boss does for his wife; perhaps you wish he spoke kinder, gentler words, like your friend's husband does; perhaps you wish his physique resembled your favorite actor's. Whatever the case, comparisons are dangerous. They make us discontent with what we have.

God has given you *your* husband—not someone else's. Respect him. Love him. Appreciate him. As you do this, God will draw you together in harmony, in love, in oneness of heart and soul.

Perhaps you're not married and you wish you were. Or maybe your husband died. Perhaps you're divorced, and your pain makes you incredibly vulnerable right now. Seek God's face. Ask for His healing, for the oil of His Spirit to be poured into the broken places of your life. Surround your life with women you can trust. Share your hurt with them. Choose to practice contentment where you are right now. Don't chase a man just to fill that void inside. Look to Jesus! Find hope and healing in Him.

THIRD, BEWARE OF THE FORWARD HEART

This step is important. As women, many times we might not even be aware of areas where we are stumbling blocks to our brothers in Christ. Although God holds men accountable for their thoughts and actions, we women can definitely help in this battle. I believe there are three areas we can guard as women.

How we dress. A couple of years ago, my parents were driving their car home from work. It was a dark, stormy night, one of those nights where you'd rather be curled up by the fire with something hot to drink. Instead, they were out on the highway, jagged lightning flashing across the sky, windshield wipers barely able to keep up with the downpour.

Suddenly, a searing white light enveloped their station wagon, they heard a bang, and then *nothing*. Their car completely died, but my dad managed to steer it onto the shoulder of the road, where they sat for a moment, thankful to be alive. Thankful they were in the car when the lightning struck them!

After a moment, they realized they were stranded and had no way home. My dad pulled on some old coveralls over his work clothes and stepped out into the torrential downpour. He attempted to flag down some motorists, but no one would stop.

Maybe I don't look very safe, he thought. *Maybe that's why nobody will stop.* So he ducked back into the car and pulled off his soaked coveralls, leaving him in his dress slacks and button-up shirt. Bravely, he stepped out again into the elements. Nothing. Car after car passed without stopping.

In desperation, he reached inside and grabbed his tie. Putting it on, he again stood in the rain. The first two cars stopped. "Oh, sir, can we help you?"

Every time he tells us that story, we chuckle. Of course, we're thankful God protected them; but for me, the real lesson is about dress: how we dress *does* make a difference. Oh, I'm not talking about dress clothes versus work clothes; I'm talking about the difference in attitude, in demeanor, even in temptation.

I know dress is a touchy subject. I'm aware of the common reasoning: *After all, Romans 8:1 says there is no condemnation to me now that I'm in Christ Jesus, right? I can wear what I want, when I want to! If it's a stumbling block to my brother, that's his problem, not mine!*

Is it really? Perhaps we've forgotten the rest of the verse. That part about walking not after the flesh but after the Spirit.

If you're a woman, I'm sure you've noticed the effect your attire has on men—the power, the pull. We have a desire in us to be noticed. We desire to be thought of as attractive; we desire attention. Is that wrong? Not necessarily, if we seek for that approval only from our husbands. However, God wants us to turn our face so much toward His that we receive our identities, our worth, and our value from Him, and Him alone.

I've been so blessed to have a husband who seeks to honor God with his eyes, who strives to guard the purity of his mind, and who desires to keep his heart only for me. What a rare and beautiful thing in our world today. How I appreciate Greg's commitment.

Let's think about Philippians 2 for a moment, that part about esteeming others better than ourselves. If I truly desire to serve Jesus, then I will care how my clothing choices affect my brother's commitment to his wife or his future wife. I will not desire to be a stumbling block. I will strive to honor God with my body.

Only God can tell you how to dress. Why not ask Him? *Does this outfit honor You?* If you're still not sure, ask your husband, a family member, or a trusted friend. Simply seek to have an open heart, an open mind to whatever God desires to tell you.

How we act. Flirting is fun. I remember doing more than my share of it in my youthful days. The tilt of the head, the twinkle in the eyes, the unspoken connection between us and someone we find attractive. It seems innocent and quite pleasant, but does it glorify God? Does it honor our future husbands—or the man we are married to?

Mrs. Potiphar did more than flirt. She came straight out and asked Joseph for sexual intimacy. However, in today's culture, she wouldn't be considered forward at all. Stuff like that happens all around us. We're immersed in a culture where women are liberated—free to be crass and bold and uninhibited. How far we've wandered from aspiring to have that meek and quiet spirit, from a heart that seeks after God, from that freedom in Christ (1 Peter 3:4).

How we talk. Be careful what you share with someone of the opposite sex. Too much openness creates intimacy where it doesn't belong. Transparency is a good thing, but vulnerability with a man is not, unless he's your husband.

Share openly with a trusted girlfriend or a family member—not your boss, your coworker, or the nice man you met at church. Guard your heart and his.

One of my girlfriends is really seeking God's heart on this. She didn't grow up in a home where boundaries were set, where reserve was modeled. She's learning now, as an adult, when to share, how much to share, and what's appropriate behavior. It's tough to learn when that wasn't taught as a child. Tough, but not impossible. God is nurturing and teaching her, just as He desires to nurture and teach me or anyone, for that matter. It's been a beautiful experience to watch God develop the knowledge in my girl-friend's heart of what to share and what not to share with the men outside of her family.

My sisters, God has created you as the crowning jewel of His creation, as the most beautiful part of His kingdom, as His own special treasure! He's put a special hedge, a special guard around your purity, around your beauty, around your heart. Embrace the hedge—no, *embrace the God who put the hedge there*. Delight yourself in Him (Psalm 37:4), revel in His attention, "pour out your heart before Him" (Psalm 62:8). Trust in Him at all times. Experience the fullness of joy in His presence, the unending pleasure of being His princess (Psalm 16:11)!

PART 6
Pride

Chapter 9

A HEART THAT *BOASTS*

I say, through the grace given to me, to everyone who is among you, not to think of himself more highly than he ought to think, but to think soberly, as God has dealt to each one a measure of faith.

—ROMANS 12:3

It had been a difficult week. Not difficult in the sense of bank overdrafts, car accidents, or mishaps, but a difficult battle of the mind. A perpetual mist obscured the face of my Father. My earnest prayers seemed to bounce off the ceiling and tumble back around me. *Where is God? Why can't I sense His presence?*

My friend Shelley told me once that sometimes God finds He can trust you with His silence. Was this one of those silent times? I knew I could take God at His Word, that I could press forward by faith, and eventually my feelings would come around.

As one day slipped into another, my discomfort grew. Why hadn't my feelings changed to match up with my faith and the truth of God's Word?

I began to plead for God to reveal anything in my life that was displeasing to Him. I knew Psalm 66:18, where David said, "If I regard iniquity in my heart, the Lord will not hear." So I asked Him to search my heart and know me, to reveal to me those areas that were not pleasing in His sight (Psalm 139:23, 24). But as I prayed, nothing came to mind.

Wednesday turned into Thursday. No change. Same mist, same sense of separation from my Father. Friday began. No change. Would it always be like this? Would I never have a sense of Jesus' presence beside me again?

What in my life was hindering Him from drawing near?

By Friday night, I finally shared my struggle with Greg. We knelt by our couch and prayed together for God to cleanse us, to reunite me with Jesus, and to reveal any sin in either of our lives. I went to bed that night with no change in my emotions.

Sabbath began like every other day that week. The same prayers that bounced off the ceiling. The same study of God's Word that didn't refresh me as it usually did. The day dragged by on heavy feet.

Then, toward sunset, the answer came. I didn't hear any voice. No thunderbolt out of heaven. But, as I sat quietly, God impressed the truth on my heart. There was pride in my life. Pride had separated me from Jesus.

TYPES OF PRIDE

At first, I thought I would address pride in just one chapter, but as I delved deeper in my study, I discovered that pride creeps in unnoticed. By nature, it is like cancer; seemingly imperceptible and harmless, it quietly spreads until one day we discover it's taken over our lives.

To me, the most obvious form of pride is the boasting type. You know, the little kid who loudly proclaims he can run the fastest; the man who's constantly talking about his brand-new Mercedes; the woman who informs you that her child is the best behaved, smartest, and most attractive kid in the room. *That in-your-face,* irritating kind of pride. However, pride is certainly not limited to the obvious. It rears up after church when we criticize someone else; it even masquerades as perceived virtues! For now, though, let's take a look at boastful pride.

BOASTFUL PRIDE

He was a middle-aged man, fairly ordinary, the type who would blend in easily with a crowd. When I was first introduced to him, I thought, *He looks like a nice man.* But his first words instantly destroyed any notion I had about his likeableness.

"I am a very gifted pianist," he said, as he extended his hand toward me. "I often play concerts, and my ability is quite extraordinary."

I politely smiled and shook his hand as he continued to carry on about his expertise at the piano, his finesse, his skill, and his proficiency. As he rambled on, I thought of the many truly gifted pianists I know. Men and women of extraordinary talent and skill; musicians who can make the piano speak and laugh and cry; people whose fingers travel over the keys with lightning precision and skill. These were the truly gifted people, yet they never spoke of their own ability, never attempted to build themselves up, never sought the limelight. Instead, they encouraged other musicians, uplifted Jesus, and turned the conversation away from themselves.

We've all met people like that gifted pianist. People who love to talk about themselves; who love to share about their gifts, their talents, their wealth; who eagerly "share" with anybody who will listen. Paul tells us, "For not he who commends himself is approved, but whom the Lord commends" (2 Corinthians 10:18).

Once there was a ruler who liked to commend himself. Oh, he had quite a few reasons to be pleased with himself. After all, he'd become king while still a young man, yet he ruled his people responsibly, fairly, and decently. He was successful in battle, he extended the reach of his country, and he beautified his capital city until it became one of the wonders of the ancient world. Above all, he was honored by God because in his court were men who feared and loved God, men who could teach him about the true God, Jehovah. He had the privilege of learning about this God from those captives, those rulers in his government.

However, despite all these advantages, King Nebuchadnezzar began to put more value on his own ideas and on his military strength and genius than on God. As he focused more and more on himself and his supposed greatness, he took his eyes off his Creator—and disaster soon followed.

In His mercy, God sent Nebuchadnezzar a dream to warn him of his folly. For a short time, he changed his ways, but then he became even more arrogant, prideful, and defiant of God than before.

One day, as this great king walked along his magnificent palace, he spoke aloud, "Is not this great Babylon, that I have built for a royal dwelling by *my* mighty power and for the honor of *my* majesty?" (Daniel 4:30; emphasis added).

His arrogance and blasphemy had reached its limit, and while the words were still in his mouth, the judgment of God came swiftly. For seven years, the mighty king lived in fields and ate grass like an ox, until he clearly acknowledged God as the Ruler of all, that He alone could give and take away, and that all glory and honor belongs to Him alone.

GOD'S SOLUTION

I believe boastful hearts never really see Jesus. We're too busy looking at ourselves and our own accomplishments to ever lift our eyes heavenward. If we were truly looking to Him, we would be transformed in character. Paul tells us in 2 Corinthians 3:18, "We all, with unveiled face, beholding as in a mirror the glory of the Lord, are being transformed into the same image from glory to glory, just as by the Spirit of the Lord."

I don't think God is talking about a momentary glance. Beholding Jesus isn't a quick fix. We can't spend five minutes with our Maker in the morning, then focus on ourselves and our problems for the rest of the day, and expect to be transformed into His image. It must be a *constant* beholding.

My husband Greg is one of the best drivers I know. He doesn't start and stop in a hurry and throw you all over the car like some drivers do. He's almost as steady as cruise control. He constantly checks his surroundings, drives defensively, and controls the car amazingly well in ice and snow. However, all that good sense seemed to have flown right out the window one day because of pride. (He's told this story in corporate worship, and he gave me permission to share here with you.)

It was one of those longer road trips. You know, the one where you climb in the car and expect to still be there twelve hours later. After a while, the road becomes monotonous. There's that certain sameness to the flat terrain, the road noise, the white dotted line zipping past.

Suddenly, some potholes loomed directly ahead of him. He expertly turned the wheel and avoided them entirely. Congratulating himself on his good driving, he glanced in the rearview mirror to see how the driver behind him was faring. Had they avoided the potholes as well as he had? Then *bang!* He hit a much larger pothole than the ones he'd avoided!

Instantly, his eyes darted back to the road ahead, where they belonged. *Ouch! That was hard on the car.* He could have avoided that large pothole entirely if he had only kept his eyes on the road ahead.

The more we look to Jesus and read about His interaction with others, the more we discern His love and peace and purity, the more we realize our unworthiness. Instead of comparing ourselves to others, we begin to compare ourselves with Jesus. What a contrast! Purity and filth, peace and resentment, love and selfishness. Oh, to be changed into His image!

When the enemy throws, "Hey, you did that pretty well!" or "You're quite good at meeting new people!" at us, we need to look to Jesus. We need to see Him in His perfection and holiness, watch His servant's heart in action, observe His care and compassion for others, and our own pride will disappear.

My friend Mollie teaches our Sabbath School class most weeks at church, and one of her nuggets of wisdom is, "What we feed, grows; and what we starve, dies." If we want to grow into the image of Jesus, if we want to become like Him in character, we must look to Him! We must spend much time studying His Word, learning of His love and goodness, of His beautiful character, of how He interacted with others. We must spend time meditating on His goodness and time communing with Him through prayer. By beholding, we truly become changed.

Chapter 10

A HEART THAT'S *JEALOUS*

I have learned in whatever state I am, to be content.
—PHILIPPIANS 4:11

He was apparently a quiet man, retiring. So shy, in fact, that when the prophet Samuel first spoke to him, he responded by saying he was from the smallest tribe of Israel and from the least family in that tribe. *What can the great prophet possibly want with me?* he wondered. But Samuel *did* want to speak with him because God Himself had chosen this young man to be the king of Israel.

Saul was his name, and, at first, he truly desired to walk in God's ways, to vanquish Israel's enemies, to rule God's nation with fairness and justice. However, after a while, pride began to build up in his heart. (His story is recorded in the chapters of 1 Samuel 9–31.) Saul's pride came out in the open when he sacrificed the burnt offerings and peace offerings himself, instead of waiting for the prophet Samuel. It cropped up again in his treatment of his son Jonathan after Jonathan stormed the Philistines' garrison, and yet again when he went directly against God's command to destroy everything that belonged to the Amalekites. Because of this, the kingdom was to be taken from Saul and given to a man who would truly obey God and serve Him alone.

After this time, I believe Saul's pride shifted to a jealous pride. Because he knew that the kingdom was to be taken from him, he centered all his jealousy on the one he saw as his competitor. Once David came on the scene and stole the Israelites' hearts by slaying Goliath, Saul's jealous pride took complete possession of his heart. Time and again, he sought to take David's life, reasoning in some deluded way that if he could just rid himself of his competitor, he would again be on top. But the truth was that he'd never really *been* on top. Yes, God had elevated him to a high position. But God was always above him, seeking to guide and lead Israel through him.

JEALOUS PRIDE

I believe that this jealous pride and the spirit of covetousness are closely linked. Like children with their toys, we see what someone else has, and we instantly desire it for ourselves. We covet the one with the most money, the best home, or the most prestigious job. In church, we seek the most important jobs, the last word, or the greatest opportunities and accolades. In social circles, we desire the most popularity, the most friends, and the most adoration.

What lies at the root of all that jealousy?

Pride—plain and simple. How often does "keeping up with the Joneses" get the best of us? How many times have we desired our neighbor's car or home or even husband?

When was the last time we could truly congratulate a fellow employee on a promotion—without wishing we had gotten it? When did someone share a story with us that we didn't try to top? When was someone able to share a prayer request or a need, and we didn't try to add to it—just to prove we knew what was going on? How often can someone share with us that they're preaching somewhere or visiting someone in the church without feeling that we need to tell them who we're visiting or about our own busy schedule? When has it not been all about us?

We all know the story of Lucifer in heaven—how he was the most glorious of all the angels, the most talented, the most important. How that all went to his head in a perfect world, we can't understand now. But it did.

I believe his pride started as a selfish pride; one where he focused on himself, on his accomplishments, on his gifts.

Then it spread to a jealous pride; one in which he compared himself to the Father and the Son, one in which he wished for a higher rank than he already possessed, one in which he desired more power, more praise, and more honor for himself.

Finally, it took complete possession of his mind and soul. His desire to become "like the Most High" didn't stay just with him (Isaiah 14:14). He managed, by artful persuasion and cunning trickery, to convince fully one-third of the angels to rebel with him!

Unfortunately, pride rarely stays just with us. It influences and spreads to other people and impacts the lives of all those around us. Pretty soon it spreads until it involves them in our sin, as well.

GOD'S SOLUTION

I believe Satan uses pride as a special enticement for the people of God. Like the Pharisees, we sometimes feel that we're above other people. After all, we don't have their addictions, we know "the truth," and we're walking in righteousness. Pride is insidious—so stealthy that we don't sense its presence in our lives until we're ensnared, caught, trapped.

The jealous heart is never satisfied. Once we have a dollar in our hand, we instantly desire another. Once we secure a promotion, we begin longing for the next one. Once five people think we're great, we desire another ten to agree with them. Always grasping, always reaching for what isn't ours.

The jealous heart isn't very pretty, is it? Yet, how often has its ugly head popped up unexpectedly in my own heart! I believe God's solution to the jealous heart is twofold, and they're so closely intertwined that it's hard to tell where one ends and the other begins.

First, practice contentment. The jealous heart is never content. Paul says, "I have learned in whatever state I am, to be content" (Philippians 4:11). Therefore, if we are truly content, we are unlikely to be jealous and grasping for what we don't have.

Contentment doesn't come easily to us—or at least it doesn't for me. My husband Greg often reminds me, "Whatever you have, Jilly, hold on to it with an open hand." Everything we have—our jobs, our positions, our homes, our families, even our lives—belong to Jesus.

Sometimes, I hold on to things or people. Somehow they make me feel more secure. But things and people can never bring security. That can only come from Jesus Christ. So as I open my sometimes tightly clenched fists and say, "God, all of the people I love the most are really Yours, and I trust You with them," then our Father can begin to grant me His contentment.

That's the key. To practice contentment, we first need a surrendered heart.

Does surrender sound painful? It most certainly can be. To be willing to say, "Not my will, but Yours, be done" doesn't always come easily to us (see Luke 22:42). But the beauty of surrender is that once we make the choice to release our own control, God gives us the victory and fills us with more joy and peace than we could ever have imagined.

Are you struggling with a jealous heart? Our Father already knows all about it. You can stop struggling. You can choose to surrender. Simply let God work in you and through you, both "to will and to do for His good pleasure" (Philippians 2:13). What I love about this verse is that Paul uses two verbs: "to will" and "to do." The Greek word for *will* means "desire," and the word for *do* means "power." So if you replace those two verbs with their Greek meanings, God is saying that He will give us the *desire* to follow Him—as well as the *power* to live for Him!

Do you lack the desire to break free from your jealousy? Does it feel good to cherish those feelings of jealousy? Go to God. He already knows all about your heart. Claim Philippians 2:13 over your life. Ask Him for the desire to break free from your jealousy.

Or maybe you have a strong desire to be free, but lack the power to do so. Maybe you've gritted your teeth and tried not to feel jealous, only to have those feelings wash over you again and again. God can grant you the power to walk in freedom!

Second, give thanks. Once you've surrendered and begun to practice contentment, you'll discover God's second solution: a thankful heart. We can choose to release what was never ours in the first place, and we can also choose to be thankful!

Have you ever met people who were always happy? Always smiling? Always thankful? Just because they're happy doesn't mean they've had good lives or that things are going all that well for them. It simply means that they've made the choice to be thankful.

One of my favorite passages is 1 Thessalonians 5:18: "In everything give thanks; for this is the will of God in Christ Jesus for you." When the church doesn't ask us to do the job we wanted, we thank Jesus that He knew what was best for us, and we practice contentment serving where we're already called. When someone else has more friends than we do, we thank our Father for the friends we have and strive to be a better friend to others. When we drive a high-mileage car, we thank God we don't have to walk. It's all a matter of perspective, really.

I just phoned one of my church friends. Before we got down to the reason for my call, I asked her, "How are you doing today?" and her answer blessed me!

"Today, I have a thankful heart," she said.

Isn't that a lovely response? To have a thankful heart and to practice contentment are beautiful things. They're not only beautiful, they're biblical— and they provide the God-given antidote for the jealous heart.

Chapter 11

A HEART THAT'S *CRITICAL*

But they, measuring themselves by themselves, and comparing themselves among themselves, are not wise.

—2 CORINTHIANS 10:12

I'd had an especially wonderful devotional time with Jesus that morning. I drank deeply from His Word, spent much time seeking His face, and now sat quietly in His presence, savoring the joy of simply being with my King. As I meditated on His goodness toward me, I began to pray Psalm 139:23, 24 over my life.

> Search me, O God, and know my heart;
> Try me, and know my anxieties;
> And see if there is any wicked way in me,
> And lead me in the way everlasting.

I had prayed this prayer often, especially in my morning hour with Jesus. Each time, I would ask Him, "Is there anything in my life that is displeasing to You? Please reveal it to me so I can confess it and, by Your strength, put it away."

This particular morning, as I prayed that prayer, God revealed the state of my heart to me. It wasn't a vision or anything mystical, but it was as if I could see my spiritual heart laid open before me. It was fairly fresh and clean looking in the middle, but pockets of diseased tissue surrounded the edges. I began to weep as I realized the decay filling those pockets represented things in my life that were displeasing to my Jesus. I had no idea what that junk represented, but I knew that God would reveal what those pockets represented to me when I was ready.

That very day, a situation arose, and my heart responded with a critical, judgmental spirit. Instantly, I felt God tap me on the shoulder. *"Jill, My daughter, this is one of those pockets of spiritual infection that I showed you this morning."*

THE CRITICAL SPIRIT

The pocket of a critical spirit not only eats away at our hearts, it often separates friends, divides homes, and destroys innocent lives. Slowly, I began to understand that pride was the root of this problem. After all, what does criticism do? It puts someone else down, so I can make myself look better. Even if I spoke nothing aloud, even if I only harbored judgmental and critical *thoughts* about someone else, they still poisoned my life and crippled my walk with Jesus, and affected *everyone* with whom I associated. How thankful I was that God was showing me what was really going on in those pockets of my heart!

This same critical spirit surfaces easily in the church. It pops out at the dinner table when the conversation turns to the pastor; it rears its ugly head in the nominating committee when someone is suggested for an important position. It manifests itself subtly in seemingly harmless conversations: "Oh, please pray for Sister Jane. She's struggling with Sister Helen—they just can't seem to get along!"

In the beginning, we're sucked in without realizing it. After all, we believe in prayer! We want to lift up our sisters and brothers, don't we? But underneath that prayer request lies something more sinister: *It's a good thing that you and I can get along well with people. Sister Jane and Sister Helen must not really know Jesus.*

There it is! That critical spirit. Always "comparing themselves among themselves" (2 Corinthians 10:12).

It's the story of the Pharisee and the tax collector all over again (Luke 18:9–14). They both went into the temple to pray. They both outwardly sought God. However, the Pharisee only did it for show, to make himself appear holy, more righteous than the common people. The tax collector did it out of the urgency of his need, out of the agony of his guilt, out of his knowledge that only his Father in heaven could forgive him and make him a better man.

The Bible says that the tax collector left his place of prayer justified, while the Pharisee received no pardon (verse 14). Why? Because he never sought pardon. He was so busy comparing himself with the lesser class and making sure God knew his virtues that he never gave a fleeting thought to his own sin, to his own critical spirit, to his own need. Having asked for nothing, he received nothing.

When I think of this story, I'm reminded of the Bible verse that says, "You do not have because you do not ask" (James 4:2). God is waiting, longing to pour out the treasures of heaven upon us as His daughters, yet we simply don't ask. We don't take advantage of the forgiveness He freely offers, the grace He extends, the mercy He bestows. What peace can be ours, what wisdom we can have, and what love will be lavished on us—if we only ask!

The Bible says that "God resists the proud, but gives grace to the humble" (verse 6). The tax collector surely received grace, yet the Pharisee received nothing. Was God being unfair? No. The Pharisee didn't ask, didn't seek; therefore, he didn't receive (Matthew 7:7, 8).

The disciples battled this critical pride often. During the three years they spent with Jesus, they constantly seemed to try to build themselves up at someone else's expense. Remember Judas and the feast at Simon's house? Mary came in and humbly washed Jesus' feet, but Judas rebuked her! He criticized her for that extravagant waste, while he sat in arrogant pride—just before he sold his Master and Lord to the men who put Him to death (John 12:2–7)!

And what about all those times they argued over who was the greatest disciple? I can see them now, trudging up some dusty road in Galilee. As always, there's a crowd of people surrounding Jesus and a few stragglers hurrying to catch up. The disciples are absorbed in the all-important work of keeping the best spot—the spot next to Jesus—open for themselves. Trying to keep the common people, the lesser women and children, away; vying for the top spot in the new government Jesus is sure to set up. Arguing among themselves about who will be the greatest (Mark 9:33, 34).

And what about the Canaanite woman who earnestly begged Jesus to heal her demon-possessed daughter? The disciples deemed her unworthy of their Master's notice. After all, she was both a woman and a Gentile. Surely, He wouldn't stoop to help the likes of her! Because of their murmuring and criticism, they nearly missed the lesson Jesus desired to teach them: we're all important to Him; we're all loved by Him—not just those whom we consider worthy (Matthew 15:21–28).

GOD'S SOLUTION

By this point, you've probably identified with one or more of these areas of pride. You might be asking God, *Please, I don't want this pride! Please, remove it from my heart!*

Don't despair! Don't give up! Don't listen to the lies of the enemy! There's hope and victory in Jesus.

Jesus doesn't reveal our pride to us only to let it slowly creep over us and consume us. He shows it to us so we can confess our sin and be cleansed (1 John 1:9). He longs to take out our stony, prideful hearts and give us hearts of flesh (Ezekiel 36:26). And He's waiting to grant us victory (1 Corinthians 15:57). Praise His name!

One of the ways He gives us victory is through knowledge. "My people are destroyed for lack of knowledge" (Hosea 4:6). So once we understand Satan's special traps, let's look at the solution God has provided for us to walk in victory.

Critical people are always "measuring themselves by themselves, and comparing themselves among themselves" (2 Corinthians 10:12). They're so busy proving themselves better than their neighbors that they neglect to humble themselves with the mind of Christ.

It was a special night for the disciples, only they didn't know it then. So they began their evening as they frequently did, arguing about who was the greatest. Now, as they sat waiting for Jesus, each of them hoped to have the best seat that night at dinner—the one closest to the Master. Each desired a special word of commendation for himself; each longed for the honor that Jesus was sure to bestow.

Then, suddenly, their bickering ceased. Jesus had entered, almost without notice. He stood there with a beautiful smile on His kind face. He sat down quietly, said grace, and they began their meal. It was their last supper together, but none of them knew this.

After dinner, Jesus arose and laid aside His outer robe. The disciples exchanged nervous glances. *Surely He won't—Jesus is going to be the King! Surely, He won't take the role of a servant—and wash our feet!*

Their distress grew as Jesus poured water into a basin and began to wash their feet. Their smelly, *filthy* feet. This was dirty work! They'd walked for many miles on dusty roads. Not only that, but this was servant's work, and Jesus was *definitely not* a servant! He was their Master, their Messiah, their Deliverer!

My favorite part of this scene of the humility, servanthood, and deep love of our Savior is found in the Gospel of John. He writes that "Jesus, knowing that the Father had given all things into His hands, and that He had come from God and was going to God" still *chose* to serve (John 13:3). For some reason, John precedes his description of the washing of the disciples' feet with those words. Why? Because I believe that he wanted us to fully understand that Jesus didn't have a momentary lapse in memory or judgment when He washed their feet. He hadn't forgotten who He was. On the contrary, with *full knowledge* of His divinity, of His oneness with His Father, He *chose* to serve, chose to humble Himself, chose to give of Himself.

The servant heart of Jesus is described in Philippians 2. Read that chapter. Memorize it. Bring it often to your mind. Remember that the Word of God has life-giving power to transform us, to call "those things which do not exist as though they did" (Romans 4:17). Even if you're proud, even if you know you have a critical spirit, don't give up. Don't lose heart! Jesus can transform your heart and write His law of humility in your mind (Hebrews 10:16). As we read, mediate, and speak aloud the words of Philippians 2, God will work to cause that grace of humility, of seeking others before ourselves, to spring up and bear fruit in our lives.

Paul calls us to be "like-minded, having the same love, being of one accord, of one mind" (Philippians 2:2). Oh, how much division and strife would be avoided if we would consider each other as brothers and sisters in Jesus. Instead, how often do we consider those same brothers and sisters to be boulders we must shove out of our way in our frantic scramble to climb higher? Perhaps we pick up little pebbles and toss them at anyone who doesn't think like we do, dress like we do, or act like we do—anyone who's different, anyone we view as a threat.

The next verse says, "Let nothing be done through selfish ambition or conceit, but in lowliness of mind let each esteem others better than himself" (verse 3). How do we esteem someone better than ourselves? Practically speaking, there are a couple of ways we can do this.

FOCUS ON THEM—NOT ON OURSELVES

We must learn to listen instead of always speaking.

Is someone telling a story? Let her share it without interrupting or trying to top the story. (I so need to learn this!)

Is someone excited about a promotion? Rejoice with him, instead of feeling sorry for yourself.

Is someone struggling because a popular person isn't her friend? Encourage her without mentioning the fact that you're actually friends with that person.

Pay attention to the person's needs. Is the person sick? Bring a meal. Offer to babysit or pick up groceries. Does he need a friend? Sit and listen. Laugh or cry together. Is the person discouraged? Pray with and for her! Claim promises from the Word of God over this person's life.

My mother-in-law Valerie (I just call her Mom) is so gifted at focusing on other people's needs. In the years I've known her, she has always been a caring, thoughtful person, always thinking of others. This precious grace of humility—of esteeming others better than herself—has continued to blossom and grow in her life in an incredible way. She's always interested in others, always asking questions, listening with her heart, focusing on their needs. Hers is a beautiful heart because it reflects the humility, the other-centeredness of Jesus. I am incredibly blessed to learn from her walk with Jesus!

GIVE OF OURSELVES—SACRIFICE IF NEED BE—FOR THEM

Does someone need a ride that's out of your way? Drive the distance anyway.

Is someone lonely and discouraged, yet you're tired? Go visit and pray with him anyway.

Is someone obnoxious and just likes to talk about herself? Sit and listen to her anyway.

By giving of ourselves, by sharing, by esteeming others as worthy of notice, attention, and prayer, we are truly walking in the footsteps of our Master and Lord.

When Jesus walked this earth, He lived to bless others. His entire life—from the cradle to the cross—was centered on others. He was God, the exalted King of the universe, the object of adoration for throngs of angels, yet He chose to lay all of that aside and come to this dark world. He was willing to die for you and for me!

Such love we cannot fathom. It truly is self-sacrificing—the very essence of humility, of esteeming others as better than ourselves.

Chapter 12

A HEART THAT *HIDES*

Let not the foot of pride come against me, and let not the hand of the wicked drive me away.

—PSALM 36:11

She was a young Middle Eastern girl; a beautiful girl, just coming into womanhood. She lived at the palace because her mother had recently married one of the local kings. Herod they called him.

He had recently imprisoned a mighty man of God—a prophet, the forerunner of the Messiah. He didn't really think this prophet was guilty, but his wife, Herodias, had pressured the king to throw him into the dungeon.

Perhaps Herodias hated the strange way this prophet dressed and ate. Or perhaps it was the immense popularity of his preaching by the Jordan River. Then again, it most likely had to do with his strict denunciation of sin and those living in sin, which annoyed her. And instead of evaluating whether the prophet's words were relevant, Herodias fretted and nagged until Herod gave in and arrested this John the Baptist.

Sometime later, Herod held a banquet for his lords, captains, and all of the big names around Galilee. And in the midst of the feast and frolic, this beautiful girl, Salome, came out to dance. She danced so well, and held those drunken men so captive, that Herod was moved to offer her a wonderful reward. After a brief consultation with her mother, Salome came back with the terrible request. "I want you to give me at once the head of John the Baptist on a platter" (Mark 6:25).

Horrified, Herod looked around his banquet hall. Surely one of those men would come to the aid of this prophet of God! He definitely didn't wish to kill John the Baptist; he had not even wanted to imprison him. Surely one of those leading men would speak up in the prophet's defense any moment now!

Anxiously, his eyes darted from one drunken face to another. Some fully grasped the import of Salome's request but merely shrugged their shoulders and lifted their glasses to their lips. Others laughed foolishly or told jokes. Still others had never liked the Baptist, so his death would be a relief to them.

Fear clutched the king's heart. *Won't one of these men come to the defense of an innocent man? Don't any of them have a conscience?*

The Bible says that Herod "was exceedingly sorry; yet, because of the oaths" made to Salome previously and "because of those who sat with him," he ordered the forerunner of the Messiah, that wonderful prophet of God, to be beheaded (verse 26). Because of fear—fear of "those who sat," fear of what others thought.

FEARFUL PRIDE

My friend Bobby once wrote an article about the fear of what other people think or the FOWOPT experience. It's the reason we let a popular person gossip to us about our friend, yet say nothing; the reason we don't want to lead the song service when a gifted singer or songwriter is in the audience; the reason we don't step out in obedience and do something God calls us to do. *Fear.* It's not always a good motivator, but it's a pretty strong one!

What decisions have we made because of "those who sat"—because of the fear of what other people think of us? How many times has fear dictated what we eat or wear, where we go, and who we talk to? Once we distill that type of fear, it all comes back to our subject of pride.

A pastor friend once shared something in passing that I've carried with me through the years. I can't even recall his exact words right now, but the essence of it stayed with me. He said, "When we feel nervous in front of other people, it's a sign of pride."

Oddly, when I first heard his statement, my pride bristled! *It's only natural to feel nervous when I speak up front. So why isn't it normal to feel scared before playing special music?*

However, the more I pondered that concept, the more it rang true.

Why do I feel afraid to play special music?

Well, for starters, I don't want to mess up.

Why?

Because it reflects back on me; either I haven't prepared enough, or I'm not very talented.

Second, the better I play, the more people will think highly of me and my ability. Does that sound prideful? That's because *it is*! There's nothing fearful about that. This type of fear is entirely self-driven, self-focused, self-absorbed. It's not simply playing for Jesus because I love Him and want to worship Him. Instead of focusing on Him, I'm focused on *me*. It's that simple.

I'm not saying you should go out and tell someone who's afraid to minister for Jesus that they are prideful. Remember what we discussed in chapter 2? Only God can bring conviction. If we try, we'll only bring condemnation, and we know *that's* from the enemy!

Simply ask God, in the quietness of your heart, if there is hidden pride that masquerades as fear in your life. Could it have been there for a while without your knowledge? It certainly pops up in my heart at the most inopportune moments! But I'm thankful God hasn't given up on me, that He's still working to show me the stuff inside.

OFFENDED PRIDE

The air felt balmy and mild. It seemed quite unusual for January, especially in the mountains of Tennessee. A slight breeze tugged at my sister's hair as we walked across the parking lot. We didn't get to shop together much. She lived in North Carolina with her husband and three boys, and Greg and I lived in Illinois. Being together was a special treat, and we were going outlet shopping at that! This was a red-letter day.

In our part of southern Illinois, shopping isn't a big event. There just aren't that many stores here in farm country. I've grown accustomed to the lack of big malls, shopping centers, and outlet stores. In fact, it helps the budget quite a bit. But this weekend was special; we had gotten together in the Great Smoky Mountains, and there seemed to be more than enough shopping in Gatlinburg!

We only had a couple of hours to get our shopping done and hurry back to prepare lunch for our families, so we started off at a good clip. First, new shirts for the boys at the Children's Place, OshKosh, and Gap; then shoes for ever-growing feet at Stride Rite; and, finally, a few stores for us—Old Navy and Motherhood Maternity—for my sister's soon-to-be fourth.

We were debating colors and fit when I glanced at the time. "Oh! We'd better hurry!" Leaving my sister to finalize her maternity clothes, I hurried out the door to check on one more store.

Then suddenly I saw him. Just a little guy. He couldn't have been more than eight. Two hands clasped tightly around his daddy's big hand. Both wearing jeans and T-shirts. They made quite remarkable progress across the parking lot, faster than I would have thought.

I knew I should be rushing to the next store, but something told me to wait. Something was going on here that I didn't quite understand, so I idled on the sidewalk, pretending to walk but really just watching their progress. Father and son. Hand in hand.

There was something different about the boy. Something I couldn't put my finger on. Did he have a mental disability? No. That wasn't it. But why were his eyes so tightly closed? Why the grip on his daddy's hand?

Then suddenly it hit me. He was blind!

I stopped and watched them step onto the sidewalk, marveling at the care of the father—and the total trust of the son.

Blind. *What must that be like?* I stood watching until they disappeared into the crowd.

At this point you're asking, *What does blindness have to do with pride, Jill? And offended pride, at that?*

Well, recently, a friend told me about one of her coworkers.

"I have never met a person who is as emotionally needy as this woman," she said. "She is constantly offended, continually needs pats on the back, and certainly doesn't see her own issues."

Have you ever met anyone like that? Someone who takes a suggestion as criticism, who perceives a quick nod as a slight, who interprets words and body language entirely differently from the way they are intended? I believe offended pride is the inability, or refusal, to see ourselves as we truly are.

Have you ever seen yourself? I mean, *really* seen yourself? Have you ever seen how you react to perceived slights, how you misinterpret what some-one says, how you're unable at times to handle constructive criticism? Has the spirit of offense ever risen up inside of you?

My friend Shelley says that the spirit of offense is the spirit of pride—and I know that this spirit of offended pride has certainly arisen in me! I've been offended, hurt, and overly sensitive at times.

I think that sometimes we women confuse a sensitive spirit with an offended spirit. Having a sensitive heart is a beautiful thing. Being open to the slightest whisper of Jesus, showing compassion to a struggling sister, taking time to hear the cry of a child are all precious graces to develop. After all, Jesus encourages us to "weep with those who weep," and "rejoice with those who rejoice" (Romans 12:15). However, being sensitive to the needs of those around us is entirely different from being offended by what others say or do to us.

When I was a little girl, my friends, and even my family, teased me constantly. At least that's what it felt like! They weren't being malicious or cruel. They simply enjoyed my response. You see, instead of shrugging off their jokes and going about my way, I *reacted*. The more they teased, the stronger my response. And my reactions just egged them on!

It was a vicious cycle, and my mom used to say in vain, "Just shrug it off, Jill, and they'll lose interest."

But I had my honor to protect. My wounded pride couldn't bear the criticism. How dare they! And off I would go, much to their amusement. It took years of unlearning, of choosing to take each thought captive to my Savior, before the spirit of offense began to rise up less in my heart.

In stark contrast to that spirit of offense is the heart of my friend Valera. She's shared how, as a child, she can remember her mom reacting to offense by quoting Scripture. And not just any Scripture! It was always a particular psalm: "Great peace have they which love thy law: and nothing shall offend them" (Psalm 119:165, KJV).

I've observed this spirit of peace when we sit in board meetings. No matter what the issue or how heated the discussion, Valera calmly sits and shares. She doesn't take offense when she's questioned; she accepts responsibility when it's given her. She can sit and discuss something that's related to her or to her work objectively. In our world of "me first," of power struggles, and of overly sensitive women, hers is a rare experience indeed! Rare, but beautiful; rare, but needed; rare, but attainable.

THE PRIDE OF FALSE HUMILITY

In my mind, "humble" pride is one of the most difficult to sense, and the trickiest to discern. This is not true humility in the sense of humbling ourselves in the sight of the Lord (1 Peter 5:6), nor is it a sense of our own unworthiness in the presence of our God. Instead, it consists of a false humility, one that meekly grovels in the dust, pretending to be nothing while really believing we are something. It's the one that looks to self and bemoans, "Oh, I didn't do a very good job preaching," when in reality, many in the congregation have just said that they were blessed by the message. The one that complains, "I'm not very good at literature," while receiving straight As; the one that says, "I'm not doing much for Jesus," while really desiring a pat on the back.

It's a creeping and insidious pride because it looks so good—seemingly humble and teachable, apparently not arrogant or boastful. What could be wrong with that? The problem with the pride of false humility is that it's self-focused, instead of Jesus-focused; it's concerned with *looking* humble, instead of seeking to please our Father's heart; it's obsessed with what *others* think of us, rather than what God thinks of us. It's entirely about self, while seeking to appear entirely selfless. Unfortunately, at times, I've caught myself in this category as well, seemingly unwilling to talk about myself, while at the same time being unwittingly self-absorbed.

Several years ago, I had a friend who constantly talked about her shortcomings: "Oh, if only I hadn't said this"; "if only I were better at that"; "if only I had worked harder on that job." However, in reality, she worked harder than most people I knew. She was very gifted in several areas, and usually spoke kind, gracious words. How sad that she couldn't truly see herself and the impact she was making for God, that she was so self-focused she never saw God at work in her life, that she couldn't take her eyes off of herself long enough to catch a glimpse of Someone else.

There's a quote from C. S. Lewis that I love. It simply states that a humble person "will not be thinking about humility: he will not be thinking about himself at all."

How true! The more I try to be humble, the more I think of myself. The more I think of Jesus and others, the less I think of myself. By beholding, we become changed (2 Corinthians 3:18).

GOD'S SOLUTION

Perhaps you've read this far, but your heart is discouraged. If so, don't lose heart! Don't give up in discouragement, for you will soon "reap a harvest of blessing" (Galatians 6:9, NLT). Our precious Savior loves you. He longs to take your focus off of yourself and fix it on Him; He longs to transform you into His beautiful character.

First, ask Him to show you your heart. Our hearts are deceitful and desperately wicked, but we can't really see what's inside (Jeremiah 17:9). Pray Psalm 139:23, 24 over your life daily. Plead with God to search your heart and reveal to you the hidden things.

And once you've asked, trust in Him to reveal your heart. I used to fret and worry about the state of my heart. Was there wickedness lurking inside? What if I didn't know what it was? How could I change it? The truth is, *we can't* change our hearts any more than a leopard can change its spots, and we definitely can't diagnose what's still hidden within (Jeremiah 13:23). Only God can do that. Only He can read our hearts (1 Samuel 16:7). Only He has the power to change us. Trust Him!

Behold Him. He was a young man, yet he'd been called to a difficult mission, a hazardous job, a thankless task. How could he endure? How would he be able to accomplish what God had called him to do? As he pondered these things, the Lord, in His great love and mercy, gave him a special equipping, a special cleansing for service. As Isaiah was praying in the temple, he saw the Lord high and lifted up, with glory and majesty (Isaiah 6:1–4). As he beheld the greatness, the purity, the holiness of God, he sensed his own insignificance and unworthiness, and he cried out, "Woe is me, for I am undone! Because I am a man of unclean lips" (verse 5).

When Isaiah truly saw God for who He is, then he could begin to see himself for who he was. Until we truly see Jesus, we'll always think we're pretty good. But the more we look at Jesus, the more we discern His goodness and loveliness, the less we find to praise in ourselves.

I believe that if we truly look to Him, we'll find *nothing* to praise in ourselves. Nothing to boast of. Nothing to take pride in. Then we will acknowledge that "all that I am or ever hope to be, I owe it all to Thee."[1]

Spend time in His Word. Where do we find Jesus? In His Word! If we're to behold Him, we must spend time learning of Him.

I know many of you come from broken homes. Maybe you've endured abuse, and the only picture you've had of Jesus was terribly twisted. Maybe you've felt that God was out to get you, or that He was punishing you. Those are Satan's lies! Our God loves you with an everlasting love (Jeremiah 31:3). He's constantly seeking to shower you with blessings. He desires nothing more than to be your Protector, your Friend, your Savior. But, if your picture of Him is warped, of course it's hard to truly behold Him, and that's where His Word comes in!

Spend time daily, even hourly, studying His Word. Start with the Gospels—Matthew, Mark, Luke, and John. Or maybe start with Philippians or Ephesians. Savor each verse. Meditate on a character trait of God revealed in a passage. Find promises you can claim. Insert your name into those promises and write them out on cards or in a journal. Keep them handy and pull them out often throughout your day. Reread them. Memorize them. Speak God's Word aloud over your life.

As you read, as you study, as you speak the promises aloud, your life *will* be transformed. There's power in the Word of God!

Focus on others. Most women like to talk. We like to share about our husbands and children, about our latest purchases at the mall, or even about our trials and victories. However, instead of always talking and focusing on yourself, ask God for a listening spirit. Ask for a heart that wants to hear, to empathize, to encourage without feeling the need to add on our own stuff.

God has blessed my husband Greg with a listening heart. Although he talks and converses well with many people, he is especially good at asking questions, at steering the conversation away from himself and toward others. He enjoys hearing stories from others' lives, gleaning wisdom from their experiences, and encouraging them if they're struggling.

Sometimes we'll come home from a gathering with friends, and I'll say, "You didn't tell them about such and such." And he'll just smile at me and say, "It doesn't matter if I tell them about that, Jilly. But I learned so much from what *they* had to say."

What a blessing to focus on others, to be swift to hear their needs, their trials, their victories, and slow to speak about our own (James 1:19).

Pray for humility. Peter quotes the book of Proverbs as he tells us that, "God resists the proud, but gives grace to the humble" (1 Peter 5:5). Oh, I surely need grace! I don't want anything in my heart that would cause God to resist me, or that would be a barrier between me and the precious face of Jesus.

Peter continues, "Therefore humble yourselves under the mighty hand of God, that He may exalt you in due time, casting all your care upon Him, for He cares for you" (verses 6, 7).

How do we humble ourselves? By looking away from ourselves and to Jesus. By looking and listening more to others than to ourselves.

Finally, guard against the first step of pride. When God revealed my prideful heart, I felt shocked, then somber, then sad. *Had that junk been lurking there all that time? Without my knowledge?* What would keep that from happening again?

After I repented, I pleaded with God to grant me discernment, to show me how to walk before Him in humility. Soon He led me on a study of pride, by no means an exhaustive study, yet He taught me much from His Word.

Our verse at the beginning of this chapter is Psalm 36:11: "Let not the foot of pride come against me." God showed me that I must guard my heart against the first step of pride—the first encroachment against humility. We are to keep our hearts "with all diligence, for out of it spring the issues of life" (Proverbs 4:23). What begins in our hearts is eventually displayed in our characters, words, actions, and ultimately, in our destinies.

Watch your heart. Keep your heart. Guard your heart.

Is there fearful pride lurking inside? Cry out to Jesus!

Is offended pride rearing its ugly head? Plead for divine grace to eradicate it!

Is humbled pride buried in your heart? Pray for the divine searchlight to reveal what's hidden.

When you step out in faith to do a work for God and fear begins to wrap itself about you, behold Jesus.

When someone gossips about you and you feel the first rumbling, "How dare she talk about me like that?" run to Jesus.

When someone congratulates you on a job well done and you respond, "I didn't do a very good job," beware! Shift your focus from yourself to the meek and lowly Jesus.

---

1. "My Tribute" by Andraé Crouch.

PART 7

Transformation

Chapter 13

A HEART THAT'S
TRANSFORMED

If anyone is in Christ, he is a new creation; old things have passed away;
behold, all things have become new.

—2 CORINTHIANS 5:17

The music swelled as we approached the refrain.

"I need Thee, O I need Thee; every hour I need Thee."

My eyes traveled around the crowded room as the women sang with gusto—some off-key, others monotone, and still others true and clear.

"O bless me now, my Savior, I come to Thee."

We held hands, and my friend from church prayed. Tears fell as we pleaded for shattered homes, hurting children, and freedom from addictions. Then peace filled the room as the women opened the Bibles we'd brought them for a study on temptation.

There were never enough seats, so my blue-clad sisters shared chairs, desks, and the floor. As each one spoke about their temptations—food, fear, anger, cutting, sex, and drugs—I was struck by the similarities: the same pain, the same emptiness, the same need to fill the void inside with junk, because they didn't know where to find healing. But while I could see some eagerly reaching out and grasping on to God any way they could, others whispered and giggled. Perhaps some even wished they'd never left their jail cells to meet with us.

It was time.

I pulled out the mud-smeared Styrofoam cups I'd brought and watched their attention snap back into focus.

The first cup was dirty, inside and out. I talked about the effects of sin, how Satan twists our thinking and defiles our hearts, then smears us on the outside like the woman dragged before Jesus, caught in the very act of adultery.

The second one was clean on the outside, but a tip of the cup showed the filth inside. I talked about hypocritical Christians and holier-than-thou attitudes.

The third cup was dirty outside but clean inside. The thief on the cross fit into this category after Jesus forgave him. Onlookers saw a dying sinner, but Heaven saw a cleansed and pure heart—and rejoiced!

The fourth cup was pure white, without a trace of mud. It represented the purity of Jesus. How He longed to change our hearts from the inside out.

At that point, one of the women raised her hand.

"I know what cup I am!" she said, sitting cross-legged on the floor, orange Crocs revealed below her blue jail uniform.

I glanced her way. "What cup, Karen?"*

"This one," she said, picking the one that was dirty outside, yet pure inside. "Jesus cleansed my heart and forgave me, but I'm still filthy on the outside."

Tears filled my eyes. What a spiritual leader Karen was in the local jail! In the past year, as she'd encouraged the other girls and studied her Bible, her countenance had changed from guarded and dark to open and transparent sunshine! No, she wasn't a dirty cup at all, but she couldn't see that.

I knelt down by the cups on the floor, slowly picked up the pure white one, and held it out to her. "Karen, you may *feel* like the cup that is dirty on the outside, but when we look at you, we see the pure cup. The cleansing blood of Jesus has spilled out of your heart and transformed your life—and your face!"

Tears welled in Karen's eyes.

"We're so blessed by your walk with God," I continued. "You reflect Him! You see yourself as dirty, and yes, you are in jail; but we see that you're free from your past. We see the peace and purity of Jesus in you."

A TRANSFORMED HEART

Oh, the glorious difference when Jesus transforms the soul! What a difference God had made in Karen's life. The amazing thing about transformation is that it happens so subtly that we're not always aware of it. Karen knew

---

*   Not her real name.

God had done a work in her heart, that was apparent to her, but the part that was hidden to her was revealed to the rest of us. Often that's how God works. As He does His heart work in our lives, it spills over onto the outside. And soon others begin to take note that we have been with Jesus (Acts 4:13).

Transformation doesn't always occur gradually. Sometimes Jesus gives instant deliverance from an addiction or a certain stronghold of sin in our lives. Such is the case with one woman I met recently. She suffered terribly from alcoholism, but God has totally removed her desire for alcohol and has transformed her life. Recently, she came to our women's prayer group, and she was excited! "I feel like God has done a one-hundred-eighty-degree change in my heart!" she exclaimed, joy radiating from her face. "The things I used to love are now almost repulsive to me. It's as if I have a brand-new heart."

Instantly, I thought of that promise in Hebrews where Paul says that God will write His law in our hearts and in our minds (Hebrews 10:16). That's what He was doing for this woman! In reality, God *has* given her a brand-new heart—new desires, fresh victories, earnest hope. What a joy to watch Jesus at work in her life!

TRANSFORMED BY TRIALS

We're almost at the end of our journey together, sister. I pray that as you begin applying the principles you've learned and spend time studying the Bible, God will bring about a radical transformation in your heart. He will cleanse you and stand you up as His daughter! I believe transformation occurs every time we say Yes to Jesus, every time we choose to surrender and do things God's way.

Every time I read John 15, I'm reminded of my husband Greg. You see, Greg loves the outdoors. Whether it's hiking or canoeing, gardening or driving a tractor, he's never happier than when he's outside. Hands in the dirt. The sun on his face, and the wind in his hair. During the winter, he pores over our seed and plant catalogs; and just as the spring peepers begin to sing, he's outside—tilling up the ground cover that grew last fall, mulching the flower beds, fertilizing the lawn.

One of his special loves is berries. We've grown strawberries, blueberries (which died), and most recently, raspberries. Our raspberry plants grow on the south side of our garage, right next to our garden. Last summer, they grew quite tall—almost to my shoulder, in fact. How delightful it is to eat that sweet, tangy fruit right out of our berry patch!

But gardens don't just grow by themselves. As I read over that chapter in John, I'm reminded again that our Father loves to garden too, except His garden is quite different from ours. He plants His Word deep into the soil of our hearts (Luke 8:4–15); He tills up the fallow ground (Hosea 10:12); He fertilizes it well by His Spirit. Then, as the plants begin to bear fruit, He does the hardest job of all: pruning. "Every branch in Me that does not bear fruit He takes away; and every branch that bears fruit He prunes, that it may bear more fruit" (John 15:2).

Does our Father prune because He dislikes us? Oh no! On the contrary, He prunes because He loves us (Proverbs 3:12), because He sees what we could become and desires for us to bear much fruit (John 15:2). He's said that we haven't chosen Him; rather, He's chosen us. Why? "That you should go and bear fruit" (verse 16).

The fruit our Savior grows in our hearts is described in Galatians 5:22, 23. It's quite a list: love, joy, peace, long-suffering, gentleness, goodness, faith, meekness, temperance. On our own, we can't conjure up love or create joy or produce peace. Our best attempts at growing those would be fake. They're the precious graces, the beautiful fruits our Father loves to grow in the garden of our hearts. As we surrender to Jesus, He's the One who grows this fruit in our lives. And many times, this fruit grows fastest and sweetest following the pruning process, through the fiery trials.

Yes, this pruning hurts; after all, Peter likens it to being in a furnace (1 Peter 1:7, NLT). But the end result is beautiful: "When He has tested me, I shall come forth as gold" (Job 23:10).

Are you in the furnace right now, dear sister? Our Father sees and knows. He's monitoring the fire, making sure it won't burn you, that it's just hot enough to purge away all of the impurities. "Now no chastening seems to be joyful for the present, but painful; nevertheless, afterward it yields the peaceable fruit of righteousness to those who have been trained by it" (Hebrews 12:11).

A friend's life is such a beautiful picture of Jesus. If you asked her, she would never say that. She would probably say something about God's incredible goodness to her or how much she loves Him, yet His character is so evident in her life. She notices when someone is discouraged and encourages her; she hugs those who hurt and prays with those who struggle. She's unpretentious, never makes a show for herself, yet her presence is always felt. She's always thinking of others, but mostly, she just talks of Jesus. Every time I'm with her, I come away feeling as if I've been at the very doors of heaven,

breathing in the very atmosphere of Jesus. What a beautiful experience!

Has my friend had trials? Most definitely. Yet, somehow, through them, she's become more like her best Friend, Jesus. Hers is a sweet faith, a beautiful trust in her Savior. Whatever comes her way, she takes it as if from the hand of her Father with joy and praise, because He loves her enough to send it her way. What a testimony of what God can do in our lives through trials, if we'll only let Him!

TRANSFORMED BY HIS WORD

The Word of God is one of the most powerful cleansing agents I know of. A surface reading of the Bible is not enough; we must study deeply to allow the truths in the Bible to purify our souls (Ephesians 5:26). God's Word has the power to penetrate our hearts, to reveal our sins to us, to change our lives (Hebrews 4:12).

A couple of years ago, something happened to show me the absolute life-changing power of the Word of God. I'll call her Sarah. She was a beautiful woman with a heart that earnestly desired to follow Jesus. Due to chemical imbalances in her brain and other factors, she'd landed in the psychiatric ward of a local hospital.

Another church member and I decided to visit Sarah to try to bring her some encouragement and hope. We talked of many things, but our talk slowed as we neared the hospital. *What can we say that will bring Sarah encouragement?* we wondered. Oh, we so wanted to be used by Jesus, to have His love flow through us to touch Sarah's life!

After I parked the car, we bowed our heads in prayer. After a bit, we picked up our Bibles and headed inside. We had to check our purses in a little locker reserved for visitors. Finally, they took us to Sarah's room.

Even now, it brings tears to my eyes as I remember our experience: the pain she was in, the absolute hopelessness, the tears coursing down her cheeks. She sat on her bed, and we sat beside her.

What can we say that will make a difference? She remained unresponsive to everything we said. We tried different tactics. We simply listened. We held her and cried. We earnestly prayed. We tried to sing. Nothing. No change.

Finally, I turned to my Bible. Opening it, I looked into Sarah's eyes. "May I read you some promises from God's Word?"

No change. For a fleeting moment, I almost gave up. *It might not make any difference,* I thought. Then, resolutely, I opened my Bible to one of my favorite psalms—chapter 91. I began to read, looking intently into Sarah's eyes, inserting her name into the verses, praying as I went.

> [Sarah] who dwells in the secret place of the Most High [and]
> Shall abide under the shadow of the Almighty.
> [Sarah] will say of the LORD, "He is my refuge and my fortress;
> My God, in Him I will trust" (Psalm 91:1, 2).

Suddenly, Sarah's eyes focused intently on my face. Her sobs slowed, and I continued reading, " '[God] shall cover [Sarah] with His feathers, and under His wings [Sarah] shall take refuge' " (verse 4).

The sobs ceased. The rocking stopped. The Word of God flowed into Sarah's heart, and brought with it healing, life-giving power, and transformation! I finished the chapter, marveling at the power of God at what His Word could accomplish.

I've experienced the power of God's Word at work in my own heart many times, but I don't think I've ever seen such an immediate, radical response in anyone like I did that day.

What about your heart, my sister? You know you're not like Jesus yet, but do you want to be? Spend time reading His Word. Read His promises and speak them aloud over your life. They have life-changing, life-giving power, for they are the very words of God. The words He's given to us are spirit and life (John 6:63). As you read those promises, know that God is at work, transforming your life and character.

TRANSFORMED BY THE POTTER

It was one of those childhood friendships. They played together constantly—in the creek, in the woods, over by the garden. They pedaled bikes up steep hills, climbed rugged rock formations, waded and fished in mountain streams. The fact that they were brother and sister only deepened their friendship, only tightened their bond.

Every time we get together, I love to hear childhood stories about Greg and his sister, Janelle. Their past was quite exciting compared to my own growing-up years. We sit and laugh over the dinner table as they recount blindfolded hiking adventures, damming up a creek, and bike accidents. One story in particular, though, deals with transformation.

It happened when they were quite young. Janelle, the younger, was still impressionable; and as they made mud pies, Greg stirred and shaped and remade the dirt until his mud pie looked very edible. In fact, it looked delicious, realistic, just like something straight out of the bakery.

Janelle decided to try a sample. After all, it must be good. It certainly looked real! However, with her first bite, the illusions of the bakery receded.

"Yuck!" she said. The taste and texture revealed that it most definitely was a mud pie!

Our Father, the Master Potter, loves to work with dirt as well. In the beginning, He fashioned Adam from the dust of the ground (Genesis 2:7). And ever since, He's been shaping and sculpting His jars of clay—you and me!

However, unlike Greg's mud pie, when God is finished, we don't just *look* like our Savior on the outside; we're the *real thing*. Transformed from the inside out. Made into the image of our Maker. Just like Jesus!

There's a question the Potter asks each one of us, His clay. That question is found in Jeremiah 18. First, the Lord tells Jeremiah to go to the potter's house, and as he watches, the potter works a vessel on the wheel, yet the clay was either too stiff or there was a stone in it—some sort of imperfection. So the potter remade it again into another vessel (Jeremiah 18:2–4).

Then, God spoke, not only to Jeremiah's heart, but to all our hearts, as daughters of God: " 'O house of Israel, can I not do with you as this potter?' says the LORD. 'Look, as the clay is in the potter's hand, so are you in My hand, O house of Israel!' " (verse 6).

Does the clay resist the work of the potter? Of course not. It's only clay. Yet how often have we resisted the work of God in our hearts? How often have we struggled against the hand of the Potter and refused to be molded?

What a privilege is ours to be molded by the Master Potter! He never makes a mistake. He knows exactly what He's doing. If we stay on the wheel, if we're willing to submit, He'll carry forward to completion the beautiful work He's doing in our lives (Philippians 1:6). How He loves us! How He desires to mold us into vessels of honor (2 Timothy 2:20, 21)!

We're really His three times over: first by creation, next by redemption, and finally by transformation. Remade into His likeness. Restored in the image of our Maker.

That's the beauty of transformation—God prunes and shapes us, washes us with His Word, then molds and fashions us until we're beautiful reflections of His character, of His love. It's all about Him. It's *always* been about Him. It *will always* be about Him. Oh, the *privilege* of being His daughters!

Chapter 14

A HEART THAT *SERVES*

You are a chosen generation, a royal priesthood, a holy nation, His own special people, that you may proclaim the praises of Him who called you out of darkness into His marvelous light.

—1 PETER 2:9

I was a typical adolescent, just breaking into my teens, pushing boundaries. One minute happy; the next angry at rules and authority. Much of my turmoil centered on my walk with God. I had been trained in the Word of God and the ways of the church, but I hadn't yet met Jesus. I hadn't experienced His peace and joy for myself and didn't know whether He could actually give me victory. So many people in my life seemed hypocritical. *Is everybody a fake? Aren't there any real Christians out there?*

Then, something happened in my self-centered world. My mom began to *change*!

To understand the enormity of this, you must understand my childhood. My mom was a wonderful mom—caring, nurturing, loving—unless, of course, she got irritated. Then she might yell, and she would definitely respond in frustration. In retrospect, I believe my sister and I pushed her buttons just to see her get upset.

Suddenly, though, her impatience began to dissipate, and soon it vanished altogether. The same stressful situations—the very ones that formerly would have made her blood boil—ceased to cause even a ripple on the surface. The frustration, the irritation, the harsh tone of voice—all gone!

I spent nights pondering this turn of events. *What has changed? Why is my mom so different?* Surely it was just a put-on.

For a few weeks, I spent my days tormenting her, pushing all the buttons that had caused her frustration in the past. Nothing. No anger. No bitterness. Not even a hint of irritation. She really was different. Vastly so. It was like night and day!

Finally, I decided to ask. I found her in the kitchen, singing. *She did that more often these days.* "Hey, Mom, can I ask you a question?"

She turned from the sink with a smile. *That was another change. She now was always happy.* "Of course, sweetheart, what is it?"

"*Um,* well." I wasn't sure how to start.

"It's OK, Jill. What's on your mind?" She pulled her hands out of the dishwater and began to dry them on a towel.

"It's just that you're so different, Mom. So happy. Why don't you get angry at us anymore?" *There. It was out in the open now.*

A look of joy flooded my mom's face. "Oh, Jilly, the difference is Jesus. I never knew before how He could transform my life, how He could enable me to walk in victory. What a difference He's made in my life!"

But she didn't have to tell me about the difference He'd made in her life—the change was obvious. Suddenly, it was clear: if God could transform my mom's life like that, I wanted to follow Him too.

THE NEED

Each day we women pass hurting people—people without hope, people desperate for help, people searching for healing, people wondering, *Can my life be changed? Will Christianity work for me?*

Where are the women who are willing to step into the gap for their sisters, happy to show them the way to freedom through healing in Christ? Where are they? *Where am I?*

When Jesus has truly transformed our hearts, I believe we will want to show what He's done in our own hearts and lives. After all, what He's done for me, He'll also do for you!

God doesn't save us to sit in silence. He doesn't transform us so we can focus on ourselves and ignore the needs of others. On the contrary, He empowers us to be His witnesses. Consider the words of Isaiah: " 'You are My witnesses,' says the Lord, 'and My servant whom I have chosen.' " And " 'You are My witnesses,' says the Lord, 'that I am God' " (Isaiah 43:10, 12).

Isaiah 12 paints a beautiful picture of the transformation God desires to bring to each of our hearts, and it begins with praise. Why should we praise Him? Because He has redeemed us, because He gives us strength, and because He fills us with His joy (Isaiah 12:2, 3).

Then comes the best part!

> In that day you will say:
>> "Praise the LORD, call upon His name;
>> Declare His deeds among the peoples,
>> Make mention that His name is exalted" (verse 4).

We will share Jesus simply because we can't help it, because He's filled our lives to overflowing, because He's transformed us so much that we desire our friends to experience that too!

If we don't live for Jesus, who will?

If we don't love others, who will?

If we don't speak for Him, who will?

THE FEAR

It was a cold, rainy day. I hadn't brought an umbrella, so I hurried from my car into Walmart for groceries. Grabbing a cart, I started down the aisles.

I saw her in the shampoo aisle. Middle aged, hair swept up and away from a kind face. An employee stopped to ask about her hand as he passed. I hadn't noticed her hand. I glanced at it and noticed a bandage loosely wrapped around her palm and fingers.

Suddenly, I felt a strong impression, *"Go, talk to her!"*

OK, Lord, I thought, *give me the words.*

"I'm so sorry about your hand," I said as I approached her cart.

She looked up with a smile, and we chatted for a few minutes. She told me that every doctor she'd been to, including the ones at the Mayo Clinic, hadn't been able to diagnose her problem. It had been bothering her for some time.

Suddenly, another thought flashed across my mind. *"Jill, why don't you pray for her right now?"*

In here, Lord? In the store? No, I think I'll just tell her I'll pray for her.

I opened my purse and rummaged for a pen. "What's your name?" I asked, as my fingers closed around a pen. "My husband and I keep a prayer journal, and we'd love to pray for you."

Her face lit up. "Oh, I'd love that!" she exclaimed. "My name is Jan."*

"Jill, pray for her right now!" There was that nagging thought again, but I brushed it aside as I wrote her name on my grocery list.

We said our Goodbyes and I headed elsewhere. Two more times, the Lord brought her past me. Two more times, I was impressed to stop and pray for her. Two more times, I refused. *I know I should have prayed when You first impressed me, Lord, but it would look awkward now. I'm sorry, I missed my chance.*

Coming out of an aisle, I looked back and saw her at the back wall of the store in the dairy section. *Uh-oh. God, are You trying to tell me something?* I wondered as I turned my cart away from her and continued toward the baking section.

Well, God, if You want me to pray with her, just bring her across my path again. After all, You can do anything, so You can easily make us cross paths again. That smug prayer did nothing to quiet the unease in my heart. I couldn't get Jan out of my mind! *How many times does God have to speak to me before I obey? Hasn't He already caused our paths to cross at least three times?*

Standing there by the flour and oil, with shoppers passing all around me, the Holy Spirit finally broke through all my rationalizations, all my excuses, all the way to my core—to my heart. God had given me three good opportunities to share His love, and I'd been too busy, too uncertain, too afraid. Worse than that, I had refused to obey His still, small Voice—not once, but three times!

Forgive me, Father, I prayed as I turned my cart around and walked toward the butter and eggs at the back of the store. Maybe she would still be there. *Oh Father, could You keep her there so I can obey this time?*

I peered down the open aisle, and a wave of relief washed over me as I realized she was in the same place I had seen her last. *Thank You, Jesus!*

I hurried down the aisle, only slowing my pace when I saw she was talking with an older couple. They walked off as I came up to her, and she said, "Oh, that couple is from my church, and I was just telling them about the nice, sweet girl I met here who said she would pray for me."

That was the opening I needed! "Jan, that's actually why I came back. I'd like to pray with you right now, if that's all right with you."

She reached out her good hand to mine as she said, "Oh, honey, I'd love that."

---

* Not her real name.

I began to pray, or should I say, we prayed together. We thanked God for the physical healing He could provide, if it was His will; we prayed for salvation for her doctors; we pleaded for strength and faith and acceptance of His will. With one hand on my shopping cart, and the other in my precious new friend's hand, oblivious to the shoppers, or the fact that we were in a major thoroughfare, we petitioned the throne of God and found grace, mercy, and help in our time of need.

Then we hugged, and she said, "Thank you for coming back to pray with me."

As I turned my cart around yet again, this time to leave God's sanctuary, I thought, *No, I'm the one who is thankful! Thankful I can still hear the prompting of God's Spirit. Thankful He didn't give up on me. Thankful that I finally chose to obey.*

My sister, is God prompting you to reach out to a neighbor, to a co-worker, or to the woman at the store? Are you afraid? Fearful of what others will think? Uncertain whether you're really hearing the voice of God?

Remember the disciples? They faced fear often. In fact, when Jesus was arrested in the Garden of Gethsemane, they *all* turned and fled. Later that night, fear of being taunted, fear of being identified with the Man of Sorrows, and fear of possible torture and death turned the cocky Peter into a trembling man who denied his Master and Lord. However, after these same men were truly converted, a major change took place.

The book of Acts is filled with the fearless exploits of men and women who turned the world upside down for Jesus. There's an interesting exchange between the religious leaders and Peter and John that reveals the depth of this change. The priests and Sadducees, upset by what the disciples were teaching, thought to teach those fishermen a lesson. After throwing them in jail for a night to bring them to their senses, they demanded that they appear before them to answer charges.

The Bible says that Peter was filled with the Holy Spirit and boldly answered their questions. Then comes the revealing verse: "Now when they [the leaders] saw the boldness of Peter and John, and perceived that they were uneducated and untrained men, they marveled. And they realized that they had been with Jesus" (Acts 4:13).

That's it! We can't witness for Jesus in our own strength and power; we can't share what we've never experienced; we can't speak for ourselves—we can only do these things because of Jesus! He's the One who tells us what to say (Exodus 4:12). He's the One who takes our fear (1 John 4:18). He's the One who empowers us to boldly, yet compassionately, share Him with others.

THE POWER

"But," you say, "I'm not good enough to share Jesus. Don't I need to be perfect first?" Or perhaps you say, "I'm not smart enough. How would I know what to say?"

The truth is, *we're* not the ones doing the witnessing. All God asks for is willing vessels and open hearts. All He needs is for us to say Yes to Jesus: "Yes, Jesus. Use me in whatever way You desire. Yes, Jesus, You can speak through me. I'm willing to serve."

Two of my all-time favorite Bible promises are about this very topic— how God can use us, even though we're just ordinary women. (How incredible is that?) In the first one, Paul starts out by saying that the gospel they're sharing isn't about him or any of the apostles, for that matter, but about Jesus Christ. He's the One they preach, the One they talk about, the One they uplift. Then Paul continues with this precious promise: "It is the God who commanded light to shine out of darkness, who has shone in our hearts to give the light of the knowledge of the glory of God in the face of Jesus Christ. But we have this treasure in earthen vessels, that the excellence of the power may be of God and not of us" (2 Corinthians 4:6, 7).

Do you see the beauty of this truth, my sisters? We're all just simple jars. Ordinary lumps of clay. Why? So that any of the gospel we share, any of the glory that shines through, and any of the honor that's bestowed always points and comes back to Jesus.

Our Master longs to use us, even though we're ordinary women—just ordinary clay pots—because only then can others truly see the power, the greatness, the goodness of our King. It can never be about us. It must always be about Him.

My other favorite verse is also from Paul, but this time in a letter he wrote to Timothy. First, he shares that there are different types of vessels: some are made of gold and silver, while others are made of wood or clay. Then he continues, "If anyone cleanses himself [or herself] from the latter [dishonor], he [or she] will be a vessel for honor, sanctified and useful for the Master, prepared for every good work" (2 Timothy 2:21). Oh, my sisters, I so want to be a vessel for honor, washed, cleansed, and ready for service!

There's a poem I love that speaks to this very verse.

THE POTTER'S VESSEL

The Master was searching for a vessel to use
On a shelf there were many,
Which one would He choose?
Pick me, cried the gold one,
I'm shiny and bright, I'm of great value,
And do things just right.
My beauty and luster will outshine the rest,
And for someone like You, Master, I would be best.

But the Master passed on with no word at all,
He came to a silver urn, it was narrow and tall.
I'll serve You, Dear Master, and I'll pour Your wine,
And be at Your table whenever You dine.
My lines are so graceful and my carvings so true,
And my silver would always compliment You.
Unheeding, the Master passed on to the brass,
It was wide mouthed and shallow and polished like glass.
Here, here, cried the vessel, I know I will do,
Place me on your table for all men to view.

Look at me, cried the goblet of crystal so clear,
My transparency shows my contents are dear.
Though fragile am I, I'll serve You with pride,
And I'm sure I'd be happy in Your house to abide.
But the Master came next to a vessel of wood,
Polished and carved, it solidly stood.
Use me, Dear Master, the wooden bowl said,
But, I'd rather You'd use me for fruit, please, no bread.

Then the Master looked down and saw a vessel of clay,
Empty, broken, it helplessly lay.
No hope had that vessel, that the Master might choose
To cleanse and make whole, to fill or to use.
Ah, this is the vessel I've been hoping to find.
I'll mend it and I'll use it and I'll make it all Mine.

I'll need not a vessel with pride in itself,
Nor the one so narrow who sits on the shelf,
Nor the one who's big-mouthed and shallow and loud,
Not the one who displays its contents so proud,
Not the one who thinks he can do all things just right,
But this plain earthen vessel filled with My power and might.

Then gently He lifted the vessel of clay,
Mended and cleansed it and filled it that day.
He spoke to it kindly, there's work you must do.
You pour out to others and I'll pour into you.[1]
—Beulah V. Cornwell

JOURNEY'S END

We're at the end of our journey now, my friends. But really, it's just the beginning. There are many more chapters to be written, more pages to be filled, and more experiences to live for each of us.

We are the chosen, cleansed, and cherished daughters of the King! We can meditate on His Word (Psalm 119:97), be filled with His Spirit (Ephesians 5:18), and be sent forth as His messengers (1 Peter 2:9).

Why? Because we love Him and long to share what He's done in our lives.

Recently, Greg and I made a new commitment to our Savior. Oh, we'd chosen Him before, but this was a special dedication. We committed in these three ways:

1. *However You desire to use us, we are Yours.*
2. *Whatever You desire us to say, we will speak.*
3. *Wherever You desire to send us, we will go.*

It's an unqualified, unreserved, radical commitment to the Lord Jesus Christ, to spend and be spent in the service of our Master, to serve Him—now and forever—come what may.

What about you?

---

1. Dr. Sam Sassen, *The Potter's Touch* (Shippensburg, Pa.: Destiny Image Publishers, 1992), 102, 103. Used by permission.

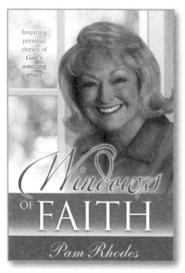